Volume 1

HOW THE WORLD
CHANGED

HOW THE WORLD CHANGED
1900–1939

JOHN EPPSTEIN

Routledge
Taylor & Francis Group

LONDON AND NEW YORK

First published in 1969 by Methuen Educational Ltd.

This edition first published in 2021
by Routledge
2 Park Square, Milton Park, Abingdon, Oxon OX14 4RN

and by Routledge
52 Vanderbilt Avenue, New York, NY 10017

Routledge is an imprint of the Taylor & Francis Group, an informa business

British Library Cataloguing in Publication Data
A catalogue record for this book is available from the British Library

ISBN: 978-0-367-77349-6 (Set)
ISBN: 978-1-00-317095-2 (Set) (ebk)
ISBN: 978-0-367-77344-1 (Volume 1) (hbk)
ISBN: 978-0-367-77343-4 (Volume 1) (pbk)
ISBN: 978-1-00-317090-7 (Volume 1) (ebk)

Publisher's Note
The publisher has gone to great lengths to ensure the quality of this reprint but points out that some imperfections in the original copies may be apparent.

Disclaimer
The publisher has made every effort to trace copyright holders and would welcome correspondence from those they have been unable to trace.

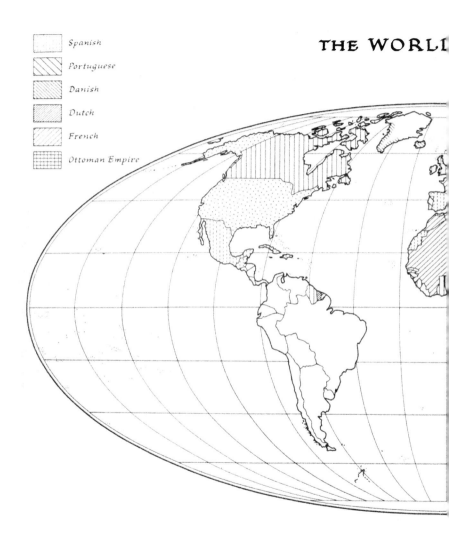

THE WORLD

	Spanish
	Portuguese
	Danish
	Dutch
	French
	Ottoman Empire

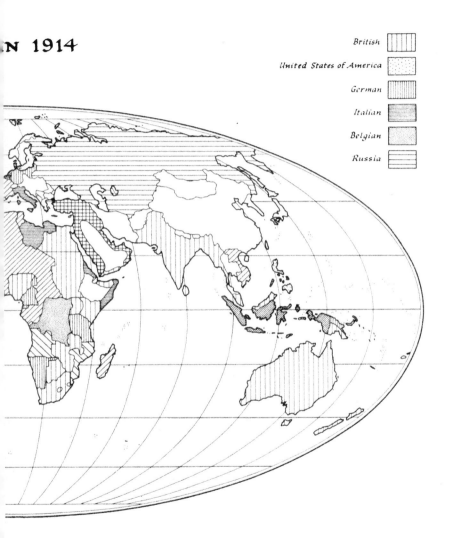

N 1914

British
United States of America
German
Italian
Belgian
Russia

How the world changed

Volume 1   1900 - 1939

JOHN EPPSTEIN   (Editor, *The British Survey*)

Methuen Educational Ltd
LONDON · TORONTO · SYDNEY · WELLINGTON
in association with The British Society for International Understanding

First published 1969
by Methuen Educational Ltd
11 New Fetter Lane, London EC4
© 1969 by The British Society
for International Understanding

Printed in Great Britain by
Ebenezer Baylis & Son Ltd
The Trinity Press, Worcester, and London

SBN 423 77670 3

Contents

Foreword   *page* ix

PART I 1900 - 1914 **The last of 'The good old days'**
1 The people's way of life   1
2 Europeans rule the world   9
3 The Chinese Revolution and the rise of Japan   19
4 'The Gathering Storm'   22

PART 2 1914 - 1919 **The First World War
   and the Peace Settlement**
5 The first phase (*1914 – 16*)   31
6 The decisive phase (*1917 – 18*)   36
7 The Peace Treaties and the League of Nations   41

PART 3 1919 - 1939 **The uneasy peace**
8 The new map of Europe   47
9 The Russian Revolution and the Soviet Union (*1917 – 39*)   52
10 Life in the Western World: economic crisis   61
11 The British Empire and Commonwealth   69
12 The challenge to democracy   77
    1] The eclipse of parliaments   77
    2] The aggressive dictators   80

   Suggested reading list for teachers   89
   Index   93

Note: a summary – for those who need it – is added at the end of each chapter

Acknowledgements

Permission to reproduce photographs is gratefully acknowledged to the Radio Times Hulton Picture Library; Illustrated London News & Sketch Ltd; the Imperial War Museum; Associated British-Pathe Ltd; Ullstein Bilderdienst; Visnews Ltd; the Keystone Press Agency Ltd; British Movietone News, Ltd; the Rank Organization Ltd; Ivor Montagu; the United States Information Service; the Robert Flaherty Foundation Inc; the Time Life Inc; Camera Press Ltd; and the Rumanian People's Republic Legation.

Foreword

Two books, of which this is the first, trace the history of the twentieth century up to the year 1968. It is the background story of the lives of the grandparents of those who are now at school, their fathers and mothers and themselves. It is the story of a single lifetime; and in that short period the world has changed more rapidly than in any sixty-odd years of earlier history. This book starts with the beginning of the twentieth century and takes the story as far as the Second World War.

Television; aircraft carrying millions of people a year, faster and faster; motor-cars for most families; the cinema; electricity in every house; refrigerators and all the other labour-saving gadgets; automation; computers: all these results of inventions which are familiar to us – not to speak of space-travel and the use of nuclear energy – were unknown or barely started at the beginning of the century. Has this made the world a better place to live in? Yes, so far as material things go, in Britain and the other prosperous industrial countries. It is very different for the greater part of the human race who live in the poor countries of Asia, Africa and South America.

Has it made the world a safer place? Progress is a mixed blessing. You might have to do your homework by gas or lamp-light in 1900 and your family might have a hard time to make both ends meet. But you did not have to fear that a whole city of hundreds of thousands of people would be destroyed in a flash by a hydrogen bomb or intercontinental missile.

But, important as they are for good or ill, the scientific inventions of the twentieth century are not the only things that have changed the

Foreword

world. More important still are the ideas and purposes of the peoples and their governments – politics, for short; for on these depend not only our way of life within national society, but also peace and war; and that means the lives of millions. During the one lifetime with which this book deals, we have seen with an interval of twenty years, the two greatest wars in world history. We have seen the Russian Empire transformed into a great power whose aim is the social revolution of the world; and the ideas of its rulers now hold sway over the greater part of the land-mass of Asia and Europe. We have seen the United States of America, which were almost 'out of the picture' at the beginning of the century, become the richest and most powerful country in the world.

Nobody at school today wants to be reminded of the violence of wars and revolutions. But history is no good if it does not tell the truth. These things happened: and they go on happening (for there has not been a week without fighting in some part of the world in the last forty years). Human nature is like that. And, if we are to understand the great changes of our times, like the fall of all the old empires in Europe and the Near East after the First World War, or the breaking up of the British and nearly all the other European empires in other continents after the Second one, we must see how they were caused.

More important, if we want the United Nations to succeed, we must look in the face the obstacles to peace which it must overcome. One of those is the *nationalism* (worship of the nation) which caused the two great wars in Europe, and which is now so powerful in Africa and Asia as well. Another is *racialism* (the prejudice of coloured and white people against one another) which the end of the colonial age has brought to a head. Another is the tussle between *democracy* and *Communism* which only time can reduce. Another is the dangerous rivalry in nuclear weapons, especially between the two Great Powers who are the champions of these two political systems. All these have their roots in the recent past.

We cannot avoid politics, national and international, because the state is the framework in which we live. But it would be the greatest

Foreword

mistake in the world to think that politics matter more than people. If there was one lesson which was driven home by the Second World War, it was that men, women and children must be protected against the tyranny of the state. The result was the Universal Declaration of Human Rights of 1948. This is one of the happier landmarks of our history. It has never been fully carried out, but it gives us a standard by which to judge politicians, governments and their laws. It is by this standard, for instance, that *apartheid* in South Africa has been so strongly condemned during the latter years of our period.

There are many other aspects of life, besides the technical inventions and politics which I have mentioned, which – if there were space – we should describe in a fuller account of the twentieth century until now. Take sport for instance. It is estimated that, thanks to the extraordinary development of broadcasting and communication satellites, 400 million people saw on TV the finals of the World Football Cup in England in July 1966. By the same means, popular tunes and entertainment have become almost universal. There has been an ever-increasing exchange across the frontiers of music, theatre, ballet and all kinds of art, science and literature. Almost every known profession and trade now has its international conference. Medicine, by a world-wide exchange of ideas and experience, is constantly improving. Interest in and discussion of the Christian religion in a changing world have been stirred, as never before, by the Second Vatican Council. All these are developments which we must not forget as we trace the bare outline of public history.

A historian must try to be as accurate as possible. What is not possible is for someone who has lived through these exciting years, as I have done, to avoid showing his own beliefs and conclusions. So when it comes to interpreting recent events, I express opinions with which the reader may or may not agree. I hope that they will be discussed on their merits.

Other books in this same series are to deal specially with international organizations, the technological revolution, and the ending of the colonial empires during the last twenty years. So I do not treat these subjects in detail in these two books of mine.

JOHN EPPSTEIN, 1969

Part 1   1900 - 1914
The last of 'The good old days'

Chapter 1   *The people's way of life*

'Mother's come 'ome' said the policeman to an onlooker who asked why the Royal Standard was flying on Buckingham Palace. That was in May 1900 when Queen Victoria, the little old lady who had reigned for sixty-three years, had come for the last of her drives through the streets of London.[1] Next January, in bitter cold, when the train brought her coffin back to London from the Isle of Wight where she died, people knelt in the fields as it passed. Everyone, rich and poor, wore black for a month in mourning for the head of the British family. This feeling of being a single family – despite many real discontents – was much stronger then in England than it is now.

And, there was much to be proud of. Many educated people had misgivings about the new Imperialism, of which Mr Joseph Chamberlain, the Colonial Secretary, was the great advocate. It had landed Britain in the costly war against the Boers in South Africa (1899 - 1902), which still dragged on and was becoming unpopular, just as it made us hated in Europe. But the bulk of the people were glad enough to belong to 'an Empire on which the sun never sets' and a wave of enthusiasm had been aroused by the legions of Indian and Colonial troops as they marched in the procession to St Paul's Cathedral at the Queen's Diamond Jubilee in 1897.

At home there was a feeling of steady progress. Industries, especially the heavy ones depending on our rich supply of coal and iron, had steadily developed, and many of the worst social results of the Industrial Revolution had been cured. Every year brought news of new

[1] From *Victoria R.I.* by Elisabeth Longford. Weidenfeld and Nicolson.

inventions. Signor Marconi's wireless system was already in operation between Poldhu in Cornwall and Newfoundland. Motor-cars were coming to be seen as something more than a comic novelty. Internal combustion engines had just been adopted for the new submarines, and an electric underground railway (The 2d Tube) had started in London. International trade was greater than ever.[1] All countries had the same gold standard for their money, and so there were no difficulties about foreign exchange; the City of London was the financial capital of the world. One could travel almost anywhere without a passport. The Royal Navy, always greater than any two others combined, ruled the seas.

There were many evils crying out for remedy, such as the dreadful slums of the industrial cities. But, for all that, life was better, more prosperous and secure than it had been in the '80s and '90s.

The old Queen's death was a great shock: people spoke of the end of the 'Victorian era'. But it did not really end; it lasted till 1914, though life became freer and gayer when her son, Edward VII, came to the throne. International rivalries and – for those who were 'in the know' – the danger of a great war increased through the short reign of Edward VII, but most people did not want to be disturbed by them; which is why he became so popular as 'the Peacemaker'.[2] All European countries except France – and the King succeeded in winning the hearts of the French – were ruled by monarchs, nearly all of whom were Queen Victoria's descendants, relations or connections by marriage.

Life on the Continent: France

What was life like in other countries? In France these early years of the century before the First World War were also fairly prosperous and secure. France was a more deeply divided country than England: the gulf between the majority, who accepted the ideas of the French Revolution (1789), and the large minority, who did not, was as deep

[1] It was not till 1939 that Britain once more reached the volume of exports which it had in 1913.

[2] 'There ain't going to be no war, for 'e ain't that kind of man', is a line from a London broadsheet of those days.

as ever. It added bitterness to all the quarrels of the period, like that about the unjust condemnation of Captain Dreyfus for spying (all Frenchmen were either *Dreyfusards* or *Anti-Dreyfusards*), and it served to strengthen the attack of the Radicals against the Roman Catholic Church. This led to the expulsion of the teaching Orders in 1903, which is why so many convent schools – exiles originally from France – are established in the South of England. But, despite these feuds which died down with the First World War, patriotism was as general in France as in Britain. Trade, industry and inventions developed with the same momentum as they did on this side of the Channel. Paris was the cultural capital of the world: those were the great days of the French theatre, with Sarah Bernhardt as its leading light, and of the Impressionist school of painters.

Germany

The German Empire was only thirty years old at the turn of the century. Several of the old kingdoms, like Bavaria and Wurtemburg were still very much alive within it. The Empire had made great progress in industry and was now the rival of Britain in world trade. Bismarck's[1] policy of winning the goodwill of organized Labour had continued after his fall from power, and Germany was ahead of Britain in social insurance (for illness, accidents and old age). By 1914 the Social Democrats had become the largest party. The *Kulturkampf* or fight with the Catholic Church had died down: Lutherans, Roman Catholics and Jews were now given equal rights. But the Prussian Army officers were a great power in the land; and what seemed threatening to other countries was the growing ambition voiced by the Kaiser, William II, for a leading place in the world. His uncle, Edward VII, distrusted him; so did the British as a whole. Meanwhile German music dominated the concert halls.

Other countries of western and southern Europe

We shall have more to say about the Austrian and Russian Empires and other European countries in later chapters. Habits and conditions

[1] Chancellor (Prime Minister) 1870 - 1888.

of life were much the same in Belgium, Holland and the Scandinavian countries as they were in Britain, France and Germany. Spain and Portugal were economically backward. Their politics were dominated by the same basic quarrel as we have described in France, only more so. There was in each a small intelligentsia or educated minority of landowners and professional politicians (usually at each other's throats) and a great majority of peasantry, mostly poor, except in areas profiting from the wine trade, or other agricultural products. This was true also of many parts of Italy, though the North – Milan and Turin in particular – had made progress industrially. Here there was a struggle to make a nation out of several old, distinct kingdoms: and the situation was complicated by the feud between the Pope and the upstart state which had seized Rome as its capital in 1870. This caused a great conflict of loyalties among Italians. Emigration from this over-populated country to the United States was now in full swing.

Industrial Europe and Green Europe

The main difference between people's ways and outlook in the western and northern European countries and those of central and eastern Europe was that the former were largely industrialized, while the latter – 'Green Europe' as they were sometimes called – were mainly agricultural. Thus education, parliaments, political parties and trade unions were more developed in the West and the comforts and amusements, as well as the evils, of town life were general. Belgium and Denmark, with a thickly populated countryside, had also successful peasant co-operatives to help smallholders. In the East, though the serfs had been freed – last of all in Russia – most of the land belonged to rich landowners with large estates, with the peasants dependent upon them for their livelihood. Conditions differed; but on the whole it was a hard life, with little chance to save and little education. The churches, Orthodox or Catholic, were about the only contacts of the countryfolk with something higher than crops and cattle, and the Christian festivals their only annual jollifications.

Cricket. Start of match between the Australian Touring XI
and Worcestershire, 1905. Note the autograph hunters

Oxford Street, London, in 1909.
Four years later the horse buses had been replaced by motor buses

The British Empire in Africa. Sketch of Cecil Rhodes
watching the shelling of the enemy in the Matabele War, 1896

Climax of American Imperialism. The cutting of the Panama Canal

Sinking of the Russian Fleet by the Japanese
at the Battle of Tsushima, May 28th, 1905

Sun Yat Sen presiding at the first cabinet of the Chinese Republic

The Entente Cordiale.
King Edward VII welcomed in Paris by President Loubet in 1905

The race in naval armaments.
The original HMS *Dreadnought* (her guns are trained to starboard)

The spark of war. Princip arrested immediately after
assassinating Crown Prince Franz Ferdinand at Sarajevo, June 28th, 1914

Paris taxis helping to carry the garrison
to the Battle of the Marne, September 1914

A British merchantman torpedoed.
Photograph taken from the German submarine

Typical devastation on the Western Front.
This was the village of Langemarck in Flanders

British troops enter Lille as the Germans retreat, October 1918

Food shortage in Germany after the war.
Queueing for the butter ration in Berlin

An Assembly of the League of Nations.
The French Prime Minister, M. Briand, speaking on the occasion of
Germany's admission, 1926

Transylvania.
Peasants in the Western Carpathians

The first international police force. British troops arrive in
Saarbrücken to help supervise the League of Nations plebiscite, 1935

Outbreak of the Russian Revolution.
Street fighting in Petrograd, July 1917

(Left) Lenin speaking to a Moscow crowd. *(Right)* Stalin

One of the most popular broadcasting dance bands of the 1920s.
The Savoy Havana Band

Progress in air mail. The famous Imperial Airways Flying Boat *Canopus*

The Great Depression in the USA
Ruined Oklahoma farmers trekking westward

Beginning of the New Deal.
Franklin Roosevelt sworn in as President in 1932

RULE BRITANNIA. Empire Day in a London School, 1923

Mahatma Gandhi at 10 Downing Street during the Indian Round Table Conference, 1931

The Great Depression in Britain.
Unemployed workers scratching in a tip for pieces of coal, 1932

Economic recovery in Britain.
The great Cunarder QUEEN MARY launched in 1934

The Spanish Civil War.
Nationalist soldiers throwing grenades

The Spanish Civil War. A family seeking refuge
during the bombing of Madrid by Nazi aircraft

In a Nazi Youth Training Camp. The instructor points to the Polish frontier, where Hitler's war of aggression started

The two dictators, Adolf Hitler and Benito Mussolini, review a guard of honour

The United States

There were two features of the United States in the early years of the century which made it different from any European country. One was the growth of huge business combines and monopolies in place of the free-for-all competition between smaller firms. This made for mass production to meet the needs of the ever-growing population and to compete in the world market. Rockfeller had standardized petrol production and made America the largest exporter of oil. Carnegie had introduced the Bessemer process and built up a powerful steel industry. Singer had made sewing-machines almost a household necessity on both sides of the Atlantic. The great purpose of President Theodore Roosevelt in 1900 was to see that government controlled business instead of the business dictating to government. His struggle was continued by his successor Woodrow Wilson; and by 1915 the battle was won.

The other great American problem was the continuous, difficult task of absorbing the mass of immigrants from Europe with their different languages, traditions and religions. Originally they had come mainly from the British Isles and northern Europe. The great Irish famine flooded the country with poor Irish. The political conflicts of the mid-nineteenth century had added a great number of central Europeans, largely Germans, Poles and Ukrainians, and, at the turn of the century, came a new influx of people seeking better conditions of life from southern Europe – Italy particularly. By 1914 thirty-five million, leaving Europe and its troubles behind, had emigrated to the United States, and it was not till the First World War that immigration was restricted, as it has been ever since. Every fresh arrival of newcomers caused friction with the older Americans. It was an immense task to make a real nation out of this 'melting pot'. That was the great purpose to which the state schools were devoted in these years, with the English language as their instrument and devotion to the flag as their gospel. The pressure of the swelling population was, one reason for the westward expansion, of which we shall tell later on. Almost all the people in the United States, except the descendants of

B

How the world changed

negro slaves in the South, had come to seek freedom or prosperity in the New World. So Americans wanted their country to be free from any political entanglement with Europe.

A new force in politics

The spread of Karl Marx's socialism became a feature of life in many Continental countries, and worried respectable people. The German Social Democrat Party, as we have seen, was the strongest Socialist party. Similar parties threw up important political leaders in Denmark, Sweden, Holland, Austria, Belgium and Norway. In France, until the eve of the First World War, the Socialists were very divided. In Italy the Socialist Party by that time had a powerful co-operative organization. But all these (whatever their theories) played the parliamentary game without resorting to violence. In Czarist Russia, revolutionary Socialism was obliged to be an underground conspiracy. There were indeed wilder spirits, the anarchists, such as those who assassinated the King of Italy in 1900, nearly killed the King of Spain and his English bride, Queen Ena, on their wedding day in 1906, and murdered the King of Portugal and his son in 1908. These were the enemies of society and the British never seriously imagined that such threats to the established order would touch their own happy island. The British Labour Party, not greatly concerned with Marx's theories, came to the fore mainly as the ally of the trade unions. In the 1906 election, which put an end to the long rule of the Unionist or Conservative Party, the Labour Party won twenty-nine seats, and the first Labour Minister, Mr John Burns, joined Mr Asquith's cabinet in the Liberal Government. This held office, with various changes, till 1916.

Some social changes in Britain

Old-age pensions and health insurance were brought in during this period. As for the schools, elementary but not secondary education had been compulsory and free of charge since 1870. But after Mr Balfour's Education Act of 1902 the counties and larger towns were made responsible for secondary schools; so many more boys and girls went to them at a small charge.

6

This was a period in which many of the mechanical devices which we now take for granted in our life made quite rapid progress. Electric light came into use in the towns, at least; also electric trams in the large ones. The Cinema developed rapidly. *The Great Train Robbery*, made in 1903, was the first film story, but by 1914 the silent films ('The Pictures') had become a popular entertainment, with a hard-working pianist or orchestra playing throughout. Motor buses replaced the horse buses in London and linked many villages, hitherto very isolated, to the market towns. It was the invention of the gramophone that probably transformed family life in the evenings more than anything else.

The family was certainly more the centre of things than it now is. Father's and mother's authority was accepted by youngsters. Holidays were family holidays, and it was rare for young men and girls to go out together, to court and still less marry without their parents' consent. Teenagers had not yet been invented. Sons usually followed their father's profession or trade. Working-class girls went in large numbers into the factories, and all middle-class families as well as the gentry had servants. Otherwise, daughters seldom went out to work. Only the Great War saw girls doing men's jobs, on a growing scale, in offices, industry, munition works and on the land. This established the idea of the sexes having equal rights, including the right to vote, for which the suffragettes had been agitating since about 1910.

Few questioned that Britain was a Christian country, and respectable people of all classes went to church or chapel on Sundays. It was the War which changed these habits, except for the Roman Catholics.

Games had always been an important part of school life in Britain, but by the beginning of the twentieth century cricket and football had become great public spectacles. In 1901, the year the old Queen died, 110,000 people – with no benefit of motor coaches or cars – crowded to see the Cup Final at the Crystal Palace between Tottenham Hotspur and Sheffield United. Soccer soon spread to other countries, and there were international matches before the World War. (On the first Christmas of the war, English and German soldiers staged an unofficial truce and played football in no-man's land.) Rugby was

How the world changed

exported to New Zealand and Australia, and was taken up by the French Army. Cricket spread throughout the Empire, especially to India, the West Indies and Australia. It was the amount of space given to sport that accounted for the mass circulation of the popular newspapers.

Open-air exercise and amusements steadily replaced many of the stuffier habits of Victorian days. Baden Powell's Boy Scout movement, which he launched in 1908, caught on like wild-fire, and, soon after the Scouts Charter of Incorporation in 1912, scouting spread to many other countries.

Summary

When Queen Victoria died in 1901 Britain was the strongest country in the world, and British people at home and abroad felt that they were one family. They also felt secure. The Royal Navy ruled the waves.

There was the same kind of order and industrial progress in most of Western Europe. There was a great difference between these countries with their town life, parliaments, trade unions and the beginnings of social security, and the peasant countries of 'Green Europe' in the East.

Socialism had become important in several European countries, especially Germany, but made little progress in England.

In the United States great business combines were becoming powerful and millions of immigrants from Europe were pouring into the country.

Every year brought news of new inventions – automobiles, wireless telegraphy, electric light, the cinema and the gramophone.

The family was the centre of people's lives and church-going was general.

Games – especially football – became more popular. Outdoor amusements replaced the stuffier habits of Victorian days. The Boy Scout movement, started in 1908, spread like wildfire.

Not many people bothered much about foreign policy.

Chapter 2 *Europeans rule the world*

The great difference between the world at the beginning of this century and the world today is that European peoples then ruled most of it and controlled nearly all the rest with their military power. The main exception was Japan, which was building up its strength; for even the great Chinese Empire, which we shall look at in our next chapter, was at the mercy of European powers who had got trading rights or bases along its coasts. This European mastery of other continents lasted right up to the end of the Second World War.

It is the fashion nowadays to speak of 'imperialism', as if it was just one big bad thing. Certainly there had been, ever since the end of the fifteenth century, rivalry and wars between the adventurous maritime nations of Europe – Portugal, Spain, Holland, Britain and France – for the control of overseas territories with their rich resources of raw materials. National pride and greed played a great part in this. During the later years of the nineteenth century three new contestants for 'a place in the sun' had entered the field – King Leopold of the Belgians, Germany and Italy. There was little left to divide except Africa, the centre of which had barely been explored. The partition of Africa into the spheres of influence or outright possessions of all these European powers had been settled sixteen years before Queen Victoria died, at the Conference of Berlin in 1885.

But by the time of which we write, the Christian conscience had been at work for a long time. From its success in bringing about the abolition of the slave trade,[1] it had led to more and more concern in Europe for the welfare of the native peoples. The idea that to civilize was the moral purpose of colonial rule was generally believed. It was not all hypocrisy. Certainly it was not on the part of the missionaries who built up practically the whole of the schools in Africa south of the Sahara, though one in four of them died of tropical diseases; or the doctors; or the many administrators who worked for years in the

[1] The Royal Navy kept up its anti-slavery patrols along the West African coasts and in the Arabian Sea right up to the Second World War.

Indian and colonial services, and more often than not became devoted to the interests of the local people. It is only seventy years since Benin in Nigeria was taken by the British to put an end to the slave trade and to appalling orgies of human sacrifice.[1] And the decision of the Belgian government to take over the huge Congo territory from the personal rule of King Leopold in 1908 was largely the result of the outcry against the cruelties to the Africans of the firms who had concessions for rubbers and other produce. So there was good as well as bad in all the colonial systems; and without the civilizing and educational work of Europeans in the past, there would be hardly any independent African and Asian states today.

There were three great 'imperialisms', in the sense of drives to extend national power across complete continents; the United States across North America, the Russians across Asia, and the British throughout the length of Africa.

American Imperialism

The British Colonies on the Eastern seaboard of North America, having won their independence from England (1775 - 1783), had inherited, as the United States of America, the British ambition to conquer the whole North American continent. The Canadians, both French and English, successfully resisted attempts at conquest, remained in the British Empire, and, after one short war, had been at peace with their growing southern neighbour. The whole of the nineteenth century was taken up with the steady drive of the United States to push 'the frontier' westward, only interrupted by the savage Civil War. A series of Indian wars had annihilated the native populations of the continent, or restricted them to reserves. Alaska had been bought from Russia in 1867, as Louisiana had been bought from France at the beginning of the century. Two wars had been fought with Mexico, and by the 1890s the Americans' 'Manifest Destiny', as it was called, had carried them to the Pacific coast.

The 'Monroe doctrine' announced by President Monroe in 1823 (and soon accepted by the British) excluded any European colonial

[1] See *Four Guineas*, by Elspeth Huxley.

How the world changed

power from establishing itself in the Americas, North, Central and South. In 1898 war was declared on Spain, as the result of passionate excitement in the United States newspapers about the Spanish attempt to suppress a rebellion in Cuba and the blowing up (or explosion) of the American battleship *Maine* in Havana harbour. This was the opportunity to carry America's imperial mission across the Pacific. After the Spanish defeat, Cuba was occupied temporarily. Puerto Rico was annexed; so too were the Philippines and Guam. Hawaii had had voluntarily accepted American sovereignty during the war. Thus the United States became, as it is today, a great Pacific power. President Theodore Roosevelt (1901 - 1908) followed this up by building up the navy and constructing the Panama Canal.

Russian Imperialism

While this American imperial tide was flowing westward, the Russian Empire of the Czars had been steadily expanding eastward. It had been thwarted by British diplomacy from spreading southward in the direction of India after the Moslem peoples of Turkestan, Kazakstan and Usbekistan had been subjugated. The extreme limit of the eastward advance, the Russian colonization of Alaska and the north-west American coast, was, as we have seen, given up in 1867. From 1858 onwards commercial and political deals with the weak Chinese Empire enabled the Russians to establish themselves on the Pacific coast and build the port of Vladivostok.

Thereafter their main aim was to control Manchuria with its great mineral resources. The railway was the great means of penetration. The Trans-Siberian Railway, over 4,000 miles long, started in 1891, was finished in 1901. Subsequent concessions gave Russia control of the Chinese Eastern Railway across northern Manchuria and of Port Arthur – an ice-free port – on the Liaotung peninsula, with a line linking it to the Trans-Siberian. In 1900 the Boxer Rising against foreigners in China gave the Russians the opportunity of pouring troops into Manchuria. It was fear of this Russian expansion which led to the Anglo-Japanese Alliance of 1902. Russia's defeat by Japan in 1905 caused the abandonment of some of these gains. It was also the beginning of the revolutionary movement in Russia. Manchuria became divided into Russian and Japanese spheres of influence.

British Imperialism

Queen Victoria had taken the title, Empress of India, on the proposal of her Prime Minister, Mr Disraeli. The administration of the Indian Empire, an amalgam of British India and a mass of princely states owing allegiance to the Sovereign, was far the most important British imperial undertaking. The magnificent Durbar at Delhi, after George V's coronation in 1911, made everyone believe that it would last for ever. A deliberate attempt to prepare Indians for a greater share in the government of their country was part of British policy, though with no clear idea of the outcome. The Government of India was the main centre of British power in all southern Asia. Aden and even British Somaliland came under it. Burma and Ceylon were part of the same domain; and the large, well-disciplined Indian Army was the main support of British influence in Afghanistan, Mesopotamia and the Persian Gulf.

The Dominions

Canada, Australia and New Zealand were in an entirely different position. These were all countries colonized by Europeans, mostly – except for the French in Quebec – from the British Isles; over nine million of them before 1914. In fact one reason why people felt part and parcel of one Empire was that a great proportion of families in England, Ireland, Scotland and Wales had relations and friends in these dominions overseas. Canada had had self-government since 1867, and Australia and New Zealand secured the same status in 1901 and 1902. They were almost independent, except for their common allegiance to the Crown.

South Africa had a more troubled story owing to the friction between the descendants of the original Dutch settlers (the 'Boers' or farmers) and English immigrants. What we call the Boer War (1899 - 1902) was in fact the third of three wars between them since the Great Trek northward of the Boers from Cape Colony in the

How the world changed

1840s. Reconciliation, it was believed, was achieved by the South Africa Act of 1909, creating the South African Union as another self-governing dominion within the Empire. One of the Boer leaders, General Smuts, was to become for a generation a hero of the Empire. Liberals in England who opposed the imperialism of this Boer War were all for generosity to the defeated Boers: they did not, alas, pay much attention to the welfare of the African majority.

From the Cape to Cairo

The imperialism of which Cecil Rhodes (1853 - 1902) was the driving force, aimed, not only at securing the newly found gold and diamonds of the Rand, but at a great northward movement, to achieve British domination 'from the Cape to Cairo'. As you will see from the map inside the front cover, this ambition for a time succeeded. Anxious to prevent German expansion and also the junction of Portuguese West and East Africa, Rhodes persuaded the government to make Bechuanaland a British protectorate in 1884. Then his British South Africa Company obtained a Royal Charter to develop and administer the territory north of Bechuanaland. This was the origin of the two countries named after him – Southern Rhodesia and Northern Rhodesia (now Zambia). Soon the neighbouring Protectorate of Nyasaland (now Malawi), largely opened up by missionary effort, was established.

Meanwhile the British (originally to stop the Arab slave-raiding) had obtained rights from the Sultan of Zanzibar on the East African coast, and Uganda, by a mixture of military and missionary effort, came under British protection. The colony of Kenya developed as a result of building the Uganda railway from the coast to Lake Victoria. Uganda in the north bordered upon the Anglo-Egyptian Sudan which became practically a British dependency since Kitchener's defeat of the Madhi at Omdurman in 1898. It had been touch and go at Fashoda in the Southern Sudan, when a French expedition had hoisted the tricolour and refused to budge. Feeling between France and Britain rose high. Eventually the French withdrew their claim and a compromise was reached, whereby France recognized British predom-

14

inence in Egypt, while Britain recognised Morocco as a French sphere of influence. This was the beginning of the Anglo-French Entente Cordiale. Britain was already in control of Egypt, though it was nominally part of the Turkish Empire. Finally, after the defeat of Germany in the First World War, most of German East Africa (Tanganyika) came under British rule. Thus the British Empire held a vast area of Africa, of varying width, reaching all the way from the Mediterranean to the Cape of Good Hope. It was the last great achievement of British imperialism. Now, sixty years after, the Empire in Africa has all disappeared, except for the unfinished business in Rhodesia.

The map shows many other British dependencies all over the world. Two characteristics of British colonial rule, already apparent at the beginning of the century, are worth remembering. One was the Crown Colony system, by which the British Governor usually ensured that the interests of the native peoples should never be swamped by the small minority of white settlers or traders, leading gradually to more representation of the former in a Legislative Council. The other was the system of 'indirect rule', which became more and more adopted in the larger African protectorates and colonies with well-established tribal leaders, as well as in the Moslem Asian protectorates (e.g. the Malay States).

The Portuguese and Dutch

The Portuguese and the Dutch were the remains of two old Empires which had no ambition to expand. Portugal had long ago lost its greatest overseas territory, Brazil, by an agreed separation. It retained Goa in India, which had been a treasured part of the Portuguese state since the beginning of the sixteenth century. The coast-line of Angola, with the mouth of the Congo, and Mozambique had been in Portuguese hands since the fifteenth century. Despite the disadvantages of weak and constantly changing governments in Lisbon, they were consolidated within their present boundaries in the first few years of this century. The railway was built from the Transvaal to Lourenço Marques, and another line to Beira. The great Benguela railway, linking the North Rhodesia Copper Belt and the Katanga mines to the seaport of Lobito in Angola, was started in 1903 and finished in 1928. The Netherlands Empire was the archipelago of the East Indies, now called Indonesia, where the Dutch had been established since the seventeenth century. They also had Surinam and a few islands in the Caribbean.

The French Empire

Second only in size to the British Empire was the French. Only a few remains of the older French colonies had survived the long series of Anglo-French wars – Martinique, Guadaloupe and French Guiana in the Caribbean, Madasgascar and Reunion in the Indian Ocean. But, soon after the defeat of Napoleon, an active policy of imperial expansion was started; and the Empire, as it existed at the beginning of this century and indeed till after the Second World War, was really the creation of seventy years. There had been a colony in Senegal since the seventeenth century, and Gabon is also an old French settlement. Trade and missionary endeavour made considerable progress in West and Central Africa throughout the last century, so that, at the 'partition of Africa', France was able to claim, often in rivalry with the British, almost all the vast African territories shown on our map.

But the most striking development was the conquest of Algeria and its colonization with Frenchmen, which started in 1830 and continued steadily. This in turn led to the establishment of protectorates over the greater part of Morocco and Tunisia, which the Italians coveted. In 1912 began Marshal Lyautey's splendid administrative and economic development of Morocco, which he continued until 1925. Just as within the ramshackle Ottoman Empire English influence predominated in Egypt and the Persian Gulf, so French missionary, cultural and trading interests were powerful in Syria and particularly the Lebanon. Here the traditional right of France to protect Catholic populations came into play. In China it was of little avail. In Indochina it had been the occasion for Napoleon III to annex Cochin-China in 1862 and within twenty years the whole of Indochina (Vietnam, Laos and Cambodia as they now are) was a French protectorate.

German and Italian ambitions

The Germans started to demand their slice of the cake in Africa in the last quarter of a century after their victory in the Franco-Prussian war. They secured, after much bickering with other powers, South West Africa, the East African Territory which became Tanganyika, Ruanda and Burundi, the Cameroons and Togoland. They also brought under their flag the north-eastern part of New Guinea, part of Samoa and several Pacific Islands.

Italy had won recognition for her claims to the greater part of Somalia and to Eritrea at the Berlin Conference. The Italians suffered an humiliating defeat by the Abyssinians at Adowa in 1896. Being determined to obtain a footing and a chance of Italian settlement in North Africa, and being baulked by the French in Tunisia, the Italian Government picked a quarrel with Turkey in 1911 and annexed Tripolitania.

That then is the picture of the division of the greater part of the world between the European peoples in the early years of the twentieth century. The United States, pursuing its own goals, played little part in the negotiations or rivalries of other empires. It had begun to have a kind of proprietary interest in Latin America, also governed by European peoples, Spanish and Portuguese in origin, in their various unstable states; though British financial and trade interests there were greater than the American. The 'Roast Beef of old England' already came, before 1914, very largely from the large cattle ranches of Argentina.

The 'Concert of Europe'

Despite the rivalries between the various European powers regarding their overseas possessions, there was not a single war between them for any colonial reason from the end of the Napoleonic Wars in 1815 to the First World War in 1914. That was because the 'Concert of Powers', starting with the Congress of Vienna (1815), remained a real fact throughout the century. It arose from the tradition that Europe had a civilizing mission in the world and that it was the interest, as well as the duty of the more responsible powers, if not to prevent war, at least to limit its effects as much as possible. Thus, even after such bloodshed as that of the various Russo-Turkish Wars, the Crimean War or the Franco-Prussian War, we find European congresses meeting to restore the situation. The Berlin Conference of 1885, and many other subsequent conferences arranged to fight tropical diseases, for instance, or to stop the traffic in slaves, arms and liquor in colonial territories, were evidence of the same common purpose. Only in the five or six years before the disaster of 1914, did the armed rivalry of the powers, finally destroy the Concert of Europe.

Summary

European peoples ruled most of the world and controlled the rest with their military power. Africa, the last great continent to be explored, was divided into European possessions or spheres of interest in 1885.

There was national pride and rivalry in this imperialism, but also the belief that Europeans had a responsibility to civilize and educate.

There were three great imperial drives across whole continents which came to a head at the beginning of the twentieth century: (a) the Russian drive eastward across Asia to Manchuria; (b) the United States drive westward across North America to the Pacific, with a claim to keep European Powers out of all the Americas; and (c) the British drive throughout the length of Africa.

France controlled most of west and central Africa and colonized Algeria. Rivalry between Britain and France in north Africa led to the *Entente Cordiale* by which they settled their differences, Britain being dominant in Egypt, France in Morocco.

Rivalries of the European powers about colonies overseas did not lead to wars between 1815 and 1914, because the 'Concert of Europe' or conference of European governments was able to bring about compromises between them, until German ambitions broke it up.

Chapter 3 *The Chinese Revolution and the rise of Japan*

In October 1911 came the astonishing news of revolution in China. This vast country, 'the Celestial Empire', had kept its own distinct civilization for 3,500 years. The traditions of government, family life and personal conduct were still at the beginning of the twentieth century those which Confucius, the great Chinese historian and philosopher, had started in 500 BC. Despite many wars, internal quarrels and latterly the success of the European 'barbarians' in opening up its ports for trade, the Empire had survived under a succession of ruling dynasties. The last of these, the Manchu dynasty, with its elaborate court at Peking, was now very weak.

In 1898 the young Emperor, influenced by Western ideas, had tried to introduce some liberal reforms. He was promptly denounced and made a prisoner by his reactionary old aunt, the Dowager Empress, who seized power and had six of the leading reformers beheaded. Both the Emperor and this grim old lady died, strangely enough, within a day of one another in November 1908, leaving a baby P'nayi,[1] to succeed to the imperial throne, with his uncle as regent. Three years later revolution broke out in Hankow and was soon in control of the southern provinces of China.

The weakness of the Manchu court enabled this rising – the latest of several rebellions since 1906 – to succeed. A strong national feeling had been aroused by all the humiliations inflicted in recent years upon China by foreigners, which the imperial government had been powerless to prevent. From 1840, when the British declared war on China about the opium trade, there had been one loss after another. In the last chapter we saw how the Russians aimed at dominating Manchuria, coming into collision with Japan's rival ambitions there and in Korea – all at the expense of China.

But though the revolutionary movement was at first more against the dynasty than pro-republican, the real inspirer of it was Sun

[1] Died in 1967.

How the world changed

Yat-sen, who was then in the United States. Sun Yat-sen, a farmer's son, had been at Queen's College in Hong Kong, where he became a Christian and later a doctor. As early as 1894, during the Chinese-Japanese War, he founded a 'Society for the Restoration of China' in Honolulu, and next year he plotted an armed rising in Canton. It failed and he fled to Europe, where he picked up, and made his own, theories of socialism. It was among his followers that the Bolsheviks made many disciples soon after the Russian Revolution of 1917.

By the end of October 1911 a truce was declared between the imperial forces and the revolutionaries, who were then in control of all the South, but not of Peking and the North. Sun Yat-sen returned to China and was elected President by a convention held at Nanking; but in order to avoid bloodshed, he refused to accept the position. On his proposal, the artful politician Yuan Shih-kai, who was on good terms with the Court, was elected instead. His object was to arrange a peaceful change-over from the old regime to the new. This he succeeded in doing. In February 1912 an imperial edict announced the abdication of the dynasty and entrusted Yuan with bringing about a new constitution in agreement with the Nanking Government. But it was not long before Yuan and Sun Yat-sen fell out. Fighting broke out in July 1913. Sun took refuge in Japan, and the National Assembly, surrounded with Yuan's troops, duly elected Yuan President for five years. He promptly suppressed Sun's People's National Party, the Kuomintang. Thus Yuan ruled the roost, with an underground opposition. This is how matters stood when the First World War broke out in 1914.

The rise of Japan

Henceforth, and for thirty years, it was Japan which the Chinese Republic had most to fear. It was only in the 1870s that Japan began to throw off an ancient feudal system. Under the Emperor Meiji a deliberate and successful attempt had been made to copy the institutions and industries of Europe and America, as the best means of gaining influence in the modern world – the exact opposite of the Chinese attitude. The British organized the Japanese navy and helped

20

to build railways. The French legal system was largely copied, and French and Germans were both concerned with army training. Americans were busy organizing education and the postal service. More and more Japanese came to study the working of factories and shipbuilding in the USA and European countries.

The result was that at the beginning of the new century, the Japanese, having already defeated the Chinese navy in 1894, were a power to be reckoned with. The British Government, realizing their political importance, especially as a counter to Russia in the Far East, made a defensive alliance with Japan in 1902. This did not involve Britain in war with Russia two years later, when Japan declared war on the Czar; but British feeling against the Russians was raised to fever-pitch when the lumbering Russian warships, making their slow way round the world from the Baltic to the Pacific, fired on English fishing trawlers in the North Sea; and there was much rejoicing when the Japanese sent them to the bottom as soon as they reached the China Sea. Admiral Togo was then the hero of every British school-girl. A new treaty of mutual defence was signed between Britain and Japan in 1905, for the purpose, it was said, of maintaining peace in Eastern Asia. It was renewed in 1911 for another ten years.

Summary

The revolution in China in 1911 brought to an end the oldest empire in the world. It had lasted for 3,500 years. A Republic was established in 1912.

The revolution was against the weak Manchu imperial dynasty which had failed to prevent foreigners humiliating China. Sun Yat Sen, a socialist, was the moving spirit, and it was among his followers that the Russian communists found disciples six years later.

It was Japan which the first Chinese Republic had most to fear for thirty years. Between 1870 and 1900 it had become a modern military power by copying and adapting European and American inventions.

Britain made an alliance with Japan in 1902 to counteract Russian expansion. In 1905 Japan defeated the Russians and obtained control of Manchuria. This defeat started the revolutionary movement in Russia.

c

Chapter 4 *'The Gathering Storm'*

It was a lovely summer in 1914. In England county cricket matches often headed the news and the usual sporting events of the season – the Derby, Ascot races and the Henley Regatta – drew great crowds. Life never seemed more normal. In spite of all the forebodings of the government and the military, the outbreak of the great war in August came as a tremendous shock to ordinary people. Why was that?

For one thing there was nothing like the general interest in world affairs that there is today. Politics, so far as they interested anyone, were internal affairs – Home Rule for Ireland; votes for women; old age pensions. There was no television to build up a feeling of crisis. Nobody thought of having 'current affairs' periods at school. Britain had not been involved in a great European war for a century, and, feeling secure, most people had a poor opinion of foreigners and their quarrels. There was no conscription, such as there was in all the main Continental countries. Even on the evening of August 1st, when Germany had declared war on Russia, King George V, that most typical Englishman, wrote in his diary:

> *Whether we shall be dragged into it God only knows. . . . At this moment public opinion here is dead against our joining in the War, but I think it will be impossible to keep out of it, as we cannot allow France to be smashed.*

We shall see later how in forty-eight hours the mood had completely changed, and why.

The weakness of the Peace Movement

If nearly everyone wanted peace – and that was certainly true of most people in Western and Northern Europe, at least – how was it that all peaceful means of preventing war were brushed aside? The 'Peace Movement', as it was called, had been at work from the 1870s, but it was small and weak. The Hague Conferences, called by the Czar in 1899 and 1907, had been a genuine attempt to halt the armaments race. But the limitation of armaments, accepted by Britain and others, had been rejected by Germany; and the permanent system of arbitration set up by the second Conference was not to apply to conflicts in which 'national honour and interest' were involved. As for the churches, Leo XIII, a great Pope who had himself mediated in several international disputes, was excluded from the Conferences because of the hostility of the Italian and other anti-clerical governments; and the national churches of England and the northern countries showed no sign of independence from their governments' policies. The Socialist International came out against war: but no sooner did it start, than all the national Social Democrat Parties – the Germans in particular – were carried away by the wave of patriotic enthusiasm. In 1908 Norman Angell,[1] then Editor of the Paris *Daily Mail*, published his book, *The Great Illusion*, to prove the futility of war to do any social or economic good. It had a huge sale: it made no impression on the military. The nation-state claimed the loyalty of everyone.

The European Conference

The Concert of Europe, meaning a Conference of the Great Powers, had been able to localize or patch up a number of European conflicts during the nineteenth century, including, as we have seen, colonial rivalries in Africa. The main reason why it broke down and failed in 1914 to prevent local wars from setting fire to a whole Continent and even the whole world, was the system of rival military alliances which had grown up since the 1870s.

The British Government clung to the very last moment to the idea of the European Conference as the means of adjusting conflicting national claims and making a compromise. Time and time again the device had been used to negotiate or sanction the gradual liberation of the Christian peoples of the Ottoman Empire in Europe – Greek, Bulgarian, Rumanian, Serbian – so as to avoid a collision between the major powers. During the Balkan War (1911 - 13) Sir Edward Grey, the British Foreign Secretary, managed to convene the European Conference, with the support of France and Germany, at the end of

[1] Died in 1967.

How the world changed

1912 to try to make a settlement between the Balkan League and Turkey, but it was defied by both sides. He tried again on July 26th, 1914, in a last effort to avoid general war, even when Russia, Germany, Austria and France were about to mobilize their vast armies and the British fleet was at action stations. The proposal was rejected by Germany.

Rival alliances wreck European unity

The conference method – the forerunner of what was to be attempted in permanent form in the League of Nations and later the United Nations – often succeeded when it was a question of reconciling, or making bargains between *individual* governments. What ruined it was the existence of secret military alliances by which two or more governments were bound to support one another, even to the point of war, against any opponent and his associates.

It was not true, as the victors claimed after 1918 – that the Germans were alone responsible for the Great War. But it is true that the splitting of the Powers of Europe into rival alliances was begun by Bismarck, the German Chancellor, after his victory over France in 1870; and that was the root of the trouble.

Bismarck's first object was to isolate France and to strengthen the rather exposed position of the new German Empire in Central Europe. First he tried for a union of the three Emperors, German, Austrian and Russian, the *Drei Kaiser Bund* of 1871. But the Austro-Hungarian Empire and Russia were traditional rivals for power in the Danubian and Balkan countries. So Bismarck fell back upon a straight defensive alliance with Austria which was signed in 1879. In 1882 Italy joined this Alliance and, in the process, gained a secret promise of support from her two partners if she were attacked by France.[1] Next year Austria made a secret treaty with Rumania for mutual support if either were attacked by Russia, and Germany and Italy soon joined in this treaty.

Thus there was no escaping the fact that France and Russia would be faced with a hostile coalition in the event of any serious dispute.

[1] But Italy stipulated that she should never be required to fight England.

The result was the Russian-French military convention signed in 1893 and revealed in 1895.

For all this time the England of Queen Victoria had tried to mainain a position of 'splendid isolation', using its influence to keep a balance in Europe and relying on the supremacy of the Royal Navy. Every effort was made to keep on good terms with Germany, though the boastful and erratic behaviour of the Kaiser Wilhelm II, especially in Africa and China and in naval matters, was irritating. It was the German naval building programme announced in 1899, greatly extended in 1907 and 1908 – that got under the skin of the British; it made King Edward and his ministers feel that isolation was not good enough. Efforts at an agreement with Germany were made in 1898, in 1900 - 01 on China, and again in 1910; but they failed.

The Franco-British Entente

Meanwhile, as we have seen, the British and French Governments had reached a compromise about their interests in North Africa. This led to the Franco-British Entente in 1904. It involved at first no military undertakings; it was really a group of detailed agreements, burying various old bones of contention between the two countries in Africa, Asia and North America. There were also some secret articles signed providing, for instance, for free passage through the Suez Canal, for the prohibition of fortifications opposite Gibraltar on the African Coast, and for an eventual partition of Morocco between France and Spain. This aroused the suspicions of Germany and strengthened the Germans' protests against the policy of 'encirclement' of which they accused the French and the British. They particularly suspected the Kaiser's uncle, King Edward VII, who had now become so popular a figure in France, of scheming for this purpose.

The race in armaments

In Germany, the army and navy did not come under the parliament, the Reichstag, but were in theory directly under the Emperor's command. This gave immense power to the military, and of these Admiral von Tirpitz was one of the most formidable. He was determined to build a navy which would rival the British. So began the race in naval armaments, with national opinion whipped up on both sides, which was only too likely to lead to a collision. 'We want eight and we won't wait' was the slogan in England in 1909. Eight meant eight Dreadnoughts, the new powerful battleships which the British Admiralty had started building and the Germans were copying. In fact in the next two years England built no less than eighteen Dreadnoughts, while Germany built nine.

The Germans were right in suspecting after the conference about Morocco at Algeciras in 1906 – though British ministers had not really faced the fact – that the general settlement of outstanding differences between Britain and France and their cordial relations would lead to secret planning for mutual help if either were attacked. It was not long before military staff consultations took place, and by 1911 preparations to send a British expeditionary force of six Divisions to France in the event of a German attack had been made. Next year came the Franco-British Naval Convention by which the British agreed to concentrate their fleet in the North Sea and the Channel, defending the French western coasts, while the French concentrated their warships in the Mediterranean. France therefore already had a potential defensive alliance with England and a similar agreement with Russia. The triangle had been completed by an Anglo-Russian Convention in 1907.

Anglo-German tension: Agadir

Thus Europe was divided into two powerful, rival alliances. Each was declared to be for defence only, and no doubt fear was at the root of each. But the competition in armaments and the prevailing nationalism of the press and popular opinion in each country produced an even more explosive mixture. Democracy had increased, not reduced, the danger of war. War came very near in 1911, when Germany, in violation of the Algeciras agreement, sent a gunboat, *The Panther*, to Agadir in Morocco to 'protect' German subjects there. The idea of the Germans possibly seizing a naval basis in the Atlantic, as they had done in China, roused great indignation in England, and before German assurances had been received in reply to a letter by Sir Edward Grey, Mr Lloyd George had made a fighting speech at the Mansion House saying 'Peace at any price would be a humiliation intolerable for a great country such as ours'. Germany did not then react to the challenge and the crisis passed.

Explosion in the Balkans

Next year, however, started the Balkan War which was destined to precipitate the great conflict. For it ended in Serbia increasing its territory; and nationalist propaganda for the 'Greater Serbia', which would include all the eight million South Slavs (Serbs, Croats and Slovenes) under Hungarian and Austrian rule, became extremely violent. This made the Governments in Budapest and Vienna very angry. There were several attempts to murder the Hungarian Ban (Governor) of Croatia and other officials. Eventually, on June 28th, 1914 Princip, a Bosnian Serb, assassinated the Austrian Crown Prince Franz Ferdinand and his wife at Sarajevo.

The Serbian Government was not itself responsible for the crime; but the Austrian Government, despite the desire for peace of the old Emperor, Franz Josef, determined to take this opportunity to put an end to the Serbian menace. Egged on by the Germans, they therefore sent an ultimatum to Serbia, with drastic demands. The reply from Belgrade was so reasonable that the German Emperor at the last moment, under British pressure, advised against war. But it was too late. The Government in Vienna had the bit between its teeth and declared war on Serbia on July 28th. General Moltke, Chief of the German General Staff, said, 'The sooner war comes the better for us'. On the 30th general mobilization was ordered in Russia; Austria mobilized next day, Germany and France on August 1st.

Britain at war on the Belgian issue

In England the Liberal Government still hoped for peace, and it was necessary to convince a very ill-informed Parliament before deciding to send the promised Expeditionary Force across the Channel. Grey

How the world changed

asked both Germany and France on July 31st for an assurance that each would respect the neutrality of Belgium, which they and Britain were pledged by the Treaty of London (1839) to defend. The French Government promptly said 'yes'; the Germans gave an evasive reply. This gave Grey his case to take to the Commons; and their response to his speech made it clear that they would make a German invasion of Belgium a cause of war. News came on the afternoon of August 3rd that the invasion had taken place, that King Albert had accepted the challenge and that the Belgian army was fighting gallantly. So let us return to King George V's diary'

> *August 3rd. . . . 'Public opinion, since Grey made his statement in the House today, that we should not allow Germany to pass through the English Channel and that we should not allow her troops to pass through Belgium, has entirely changed; now everyone is for war and helping our friends. Orders for the mobilisation of the army will be issued at once'. August 4th. 'I held a Council at 10.45 (a.m.) to declare War with Germany. It is a terrible catastrophe but it is not our fault. . . . When they heard that War had been declared the excitement (of the crowds) increased and it was a never to be forgotten sight when May[1] and I with David[2] went on to the balcony; the cheering was terrific. Please God it will soon be over'. . . .*

Summary

The system of rival military alliances in Europe made it impossible for those who wanted peace to prevent the First World War.

Germany started this system by its defensive alliance with Austria-Hungary. This led to the Russian and French military convention. Britain and France, having made the *Entente* to settle their own differences, became nervous of Germany. Britain made a defensive agreement with Russian in 1907.

The German decision to build a big navy roused popular feeling in England and led from 1909 to a race in naval armaments.

Thus two great groups in Europe were bound to go to war, if any one

[1] Queen Mary.
[2] The Prince of Wales, afterwards King Edward VIII.

of their members were attacked. The European Conference had often been able to patch up conflicts or restore peace between individual countries. It broke down under this system of automatic military alliances, though the British tried to use it to the last.

The spark which set Europe ablaze was the murder of the Austrian Crown Prince by a Serbian in July 1914. The Austrian Government, encouraged by the German General Staff, was determined to put an end to the agitation for uniting the South Slavs of Hungary and Austria with the Serbs in a 'Greater Serbia'.

Russia, as the protector of the Slav peoples, took the Serbian side – and mobilized its huge conscript army. So did the Austrians, Germans and French.

It was the invasion of Belgium by the German army, advancing into France, that caused Britain to declare war on Germany on August 4th, 1914.

Part 2 1914 - 1919
The First World War
and the Peace Settlement

Chapter 5 *The first phase 1914 - 1916*

But the war was not soon over, though people on both sides expected victory within a matter of weeks. It lasted for more than four years and cost the lives of over ten million fighting men, let alone the uncounted civilian dead. It developed into one long wrestling match, one side trying to wear down the other one, till America's entry into the war on the Allied side turned the scales.

Nationalism

Before we give an outline of the fighting, let us have a look at a few general aspects of this greatest of all wars, as it then was. First, what were they all fighting for? Towards the end of the war the Americans brought not only arms, men and wealth, but slogans, to Europe. President Wilson declared that it was 'A war to make the world safe for Democracy'. But nobody on either side in 1914 had any idea of fighting for or against Democracy, whatever that meant. The whole driving force and purpose of the fighting men, including hundreds of thousands who joined the forces voluntarily in Britain before conscription, was *national*. 'Your King and country need you' seems old-fashioned now; it did not then. The Germans had been led to believe that Germany was encircled by enemies, and their leaders certainly had proud ambitions. The Austrians and Hungarians started the war to protect their countries against rebellion and intrigue by the South Slavs. The Serbs, for just the opposite reason, soon found themselves fighting for their lives to defend their fatherland. The great mass of Russian peasant soldiers had an old instinct of religious patriotism and believed that they must help their fellow Slavs against German aggression. The Belgians and French had no choice but to fight for national survival against a powerful invader. The British were brought into war by an appeal to national honour, namely that they could not let Belgium and France down; but in reality a feeling of national self-defence was just as strong on our side of the Channel as on the other, and more than ever so when German submarines were sinking our ships by the score. The Italians eventually came into the war, after changing sides, for what the Italian nation could get out of it. And this nationalism was even stronger and more popular in the Danubian and Balkan countries and the Middle East. In fact it became the main weapon in the hands of the American, British and French leaders for breaking up the Austrian and Turkish Empires.

Total war

Another point to remember is that the 1914-18 war was the first case of *total* war, at least in European history. Compulsory military service brought all able-bodied men into the armies and navies.[1] This was adopted in nearly all countries after the 1870 war and in 1916 in Britain. This not only meant the mobilization of millions within a few days. As the war progressed, the *whole* population was involved, the production of munitions became the greatest industry, and women and girls took the place of men in the factories and the fields. Among the results of this were a distortion of the economic life of each country, the weakening of family life and a great increase in the powers of government. A whole generation of the best young men, who could have been the leaders of their countries, was wiped out. In England this was especially true of those who volunteered for service in the first two years of the war, before conscription came in. In France and Germany a fifth of all the men between twenty and forty were killed.

A third point to remember for an understanding of these years is how the propaganda of hatred developed. In order to whip up and

[1] The air-forces, created and developed during the war, started as branches of the armies and navies.

32

keep up resolution against the enemy for four long years, when there seemed no end in sight of the dreadful casualty lists, politicians and journalists in every country over-simplified the issues, exaggerated – and sometimes invented – the atrocities of the other side as if they were devils. Soldiers at the front were the least impressed by this propaganda; they were often astonished when they came on leave to discover the savagery of their aunts! This organization of hate became a feature of future wars.

Starting with Europe, the war soon engulfed a great part of the world. At first the belligerents were, on the side of *Entente*, France, Russia, Britain, Serbia and Belgium, and on the other side, which came to be called the *Central Powers*, the two Empires of Germany and Austria-Hungary. It is important to remember that the whole of the British Empire, including India and the self-governing Dominions, was involved from the start, and so was the French Empire. So many Canadians, Australians and New Zealanders fought and died in Europe, and South Africans in the East African campaign. The war spread automatically to Africa and Oceania where the Germans had colonies. Japan declared war on Germany in August 1914, but in November the Germans persuaded Turkey to come in on their side. In 1915 Italy, having been neutral at the start, joined the Entente, having obtained its price by the secret Treaty of London.[1] Next Bulgaria joined the Central Powers, while in 1916 Rumania, in the hope of annexing Transylvania, declared war on Austria-Hungary. In the same year Germany declared war on Portugal, which had requisitioned a number of German ships with British support. Finally, for reasons which we shall see in the next chapter, the United States went to war with Germany in April 1917.

The Schlieffen plan fails

The war started with Germany fighting on two fronts. In the East an immense Russian army, mobilized more quickly than the German

[1] The exclusion of the Pope from the peace settlement and, in the event of victory, the annexation of the South Tyrol, Istria and Dalmatia from Austria-Hungary, and a zone of influence in Turkey.

How the world changed

General Staff anticipated, poured into East Prussia and another into Austrian Galicia. Meanwhile in the West the Germans, carrying out the famous Schlieffen plan (Schlieffen was a former German Chief of Staff), drove through Belgium with the aim of encircling Paris. The British fought a rearguard action at Mons, the French at Charleroi, and the Belgians, holding the fortress of Antwerp, tied up two German army corps. But there was no holding the advancing Germans, till three of their armies were south of the River Marne and the advance guard at Meaux, within twenty miles of Paris.

Yet their plan had gone awry and they failed to encircle the city from the west, partly owing to bad communications between the army commanders, partly because Moltke, the German Chief of Staff, had had to withdraw two more army corps to help stem the Russian advance. On 6th September, the French Commander, General Joffre, ordered a great counter-attack. Gallieni, Military Governor of Paris, rushed up all available troops from the capital, some in requisitioned taxicabs. General Foch[1] held a furious German attack further east; meanwhile the English and Belgians attacked the north-western part of the German salient. As a result a general retreat was ordered. The German armies fell back to the River Aisne and also shortened their line running southward from near Lille. Paris was saved and was never again in serious danger.

On the other hand the advance of the Russians into East Prussia was defeated. They suffered huge losses first at Tannenberg at the end of August, then at the Mazurian Lakes, though they had broken the Austrian front. There were more furious battles next year, but by September 1915 the Russians had to fall back on the River Beresina. Yet, thought they had by then lost a million and a half men, they had a seemingly inexhaustible supply of manpower and showed no signs of wanting to make peace.

Beginning of trench warfare

On the Western front, which both sides knew to be decisive, the retreat to the Aisne was the end of the 'war of movement'. Both sides

[1] He was to be made Supreme Commander of the Allies in 1918.

34

'dug themselves in', and the rest of the war was a matter of trench warfare broken by violent offensives, costly in lives, on one side and the other, with ever more intensive artillery barrages as the production of guns and shells increased.

1915 was a bad year for the Allies – as the Powers of the Entente were called. The British attempt to force the Dardanelles and reach Constantinople (Istanbul) failed disastrously. Serbia was overrun. The war at sea became more important. The British extended their blockade to all merchandise destined for Germany, in neutral as well as enemy ships. This upset the neutrals, including the United States; but the torpedoing of merchant ships by German submarines irritated them even more, and for a time American protests had some effect in reducing the sinkings. But not for long; and the loss of allied shipping increased.

1916 was a year of heavy losses of life, resulting from the attempts of both sides to wear one another down: the Germans by incessant attacks for ten months on the fortified city of Verdun, where they hoped to bleed the French army to death; the British and French by a great offensive on the Somme lasting from July to September.

Meanwhile the only great sea battle of the war had been fought in May between the British and German fleets off Jutland. There again the result was a draw, but the German battle fleet never again came out from the shelter of the Baltic and the Kiel Canal to fight.

There was a growing weariness with the war which seemed to make no progress. The casualty lists were heavier than ever. In Ireland, there was a rebellion at Easter, 1916, and this tied down a good many English troops. As against this, the British had used tanks for the first time on the Somme, and their extraordinary output of munitions, as well as the rapid growth of their Air Force, began to impress the Germans. The Russian General Brussilov directed a successful offensive against the Austrians in the summer, driving deep into Austrian Poland, and the Italians had their first successes against the Austrians in the Isonso area.

So matters stood at the end of 1916.

How the world changed

Summary

At the first the countries who went to war were, on the one side, France and Britain, with their Empires, Russia, Serbia and Belgium (the Entente); Germany and Austria-Hungary (the Central Powers) on the other side.

Soon Japan and Italy joined the Entente; Turkey and Bulgaria joined the Central Powers. In 1916 Rumania declared war on Austria. In 1916 Germany declared war on Portugal, and finally the United States came in on the Entente side. So did Greece at the last moment.

National patriotism was really the purpose for which the peoples of all these countries fought. As the war went on, other nations used it as a means of gaining independence from the Austrian, Russian and Turkish Empires.

In the first two years there was no sign of victory on either side. The war developed into a slogging match, each side trying to wear the other down. On the Western front the armies faced one another in trenches, from which great attacks were launched from time to time.

In 1916 the Germans attacked the French for ten months at Verdun. The British and French counter-attacked from July to September on the river Somme. Hundreds of thousands of men were killed in these offensives.

Chapter 6 *The decisive phase*

The war dragged on for nearly two years more. On the Western front there was still stalemate. Towards the end of 1917 the British defeated the Turks in Palestine and General Allenby took Jerusalem. The most important development was in the war at sea. The British blockade practically stopped food and raw materials from reaching Germany from overseas: only the oil from occupied Rumania kept the German air-force and transport supplied. The Germans on their side intensified their submarine campaign, sinking at sight all merchantmen making for British, French and Italian ports.

Three events of 1917 were destined to have dramatic results for the future of the world. The first was the Russian Revolution; the second was the decision of the United States to come out of its isolation and join in the war; the third was the Balfour Declaration promising support for a Jewish national home in Palestine.

The first democratic Revolution in Russia, which forced the Czar to abdicate, occurred in March 1917; the Bolsheviks seized power in November. This will be described in Chapter 9. Within five weeks an armistice was signed between the Bolsheviks and the German Empire, and, when the Peace Treaty was signed at Brest Litovsk in March 1918, the Germans could look forward to controlling vast resources of coal, iron and grain in the Ukraine, Poland and Byelorussia. This was a tremendous blow for the Entente; for, with the Russian army knocked out of the war, the German General Staff could concentrate almost all their forces for a crushing blow in the West, before the Americans arrived in strength in Europe to reinforce the Allies.

The United States goes to war

It was within three weeks of the original Russian Revolution that President Wilson, a pacifist, who had tried all along to keep his great country neutral, asked the Congress of the United States to approve a declaration of war on Germany. Both Houses approved on April 6th, 1917. What finally caused the break was mounting anger at the recklessness of the German submarine campaign. An increasing number of American ships were torpedoed. Between January and August 1917, the Allies lost four and a half million tons of shipping.

It took a year before the United States, which had to raise and train a vast army from scratch, could have much effect upon the land fighting in Europe. But during that time priceless help was given to the Allies' cause by the rapid building both of merchantmen and warships in American yards. Meanwhile, the Royal Navy, now aided by the Americans, developed the system of escorting ships in convoy and attacked and sank many more of the U Boats. By the end of the war the British and Americans between them had safely transported over two million American troops to Europe.

After the war, as we shall see, the United States once more tried

How the world changed

to isolate itself from European entanglements. But a large minority of Americans did not accept the idea that their great country could contract out of defending the peace, and turn its back on Europe. They were proved right when Germany and its allies challenged American principles and interests even more crudely in the Second World War.

The promise of a Jewish national home

The third event of 1917 which was to be of far-reaching importance was a letter sent by Mr Arthur Balfour, the British Foreign Secretary, on November 2nd, 1917, to Lord Rothschild, leader of the Zionists, to say that the British Government would do its best to help establish a national home for the Jews in Palestine on the understanding that the rights of non-Jewish inhabitants of that country were respected. At the time this seemed to be just one of many ways in which the hard-pressed Allied governments were trying to defeat their enemies, by winning the support of particular national groups with rosy promises – like the secret promises made to Italy to buy its support; or the backing of Czechs, Serbs and Rumanians against Austria-Hungary. In this case, however, it was not only a matter of satisfying large bodies of Jews in Russia, Germany and the United States. Mr Balfour and the Prime Minister, Mr Lloyd George, were themselves friends of the Zionist cause. In the event they started a bitter feud between Israel and the Arabs in the Middle East, which has already led to three wars in twenty years and shows no sign of abating.

There were many signs of war-weariness in 1917 and several attempts to secure a compromise peace. The Russian revolutionaries, having gained power on a programme of peace with Germany, sent emissaries to the Socialists in all the allied countries to try to persuade them to take the same line. A conference in neutral Stockholm was called for this purpose. The British Trade Union Congress refused to attend, but some French Socialists went and their party withdrew from the *Union sacrée*, the coalition government. There were mutinies in several French regiments. Powerful support appeared in the German *Reichstag* for a negotiated peace without annexations. Proposals for peace came from Charles I, the new Emperor of Austria, who realized the danger of his Empire breaking to pieces. In August Pope Benedict XV sent a note to all belligerent governments proposing peace on the basis of Polish independence, the German restoration of Belgium and all other occupied territories, mutual disarmament, the establishment of a society of nations, and arbitration. President Wilson, freshly embattled, would not agree to peace without victory. Nor at the time would the German General Staff, who stamped out strikes in the factories, consider a negotiated peace. As against these feelers for peace, a much more vigorous effort was made by the Allied governments to mobilize their people for victory. In Britain Lloyd George headed the Government and in France, Clémenceau, 'the Tiger' as he was called, came to power.

So the scene was set for a final trial of strength in 1918. In March, Ludendorff, the German Chief of Staff, made a last attempt to snatch victory before the ever-growing might of American arms and men could tell decisively. He launched a sudden offensive, first at the junction of the British and French armies in Picardy, then against the French near Rheims. The British retreated for a short distance beyond the River Lys, but held on. The French, taken by surprise, did not stop the Germans till they had once more reached the Marne. This grave crisis at last pulled the bickering French and British together and persuaded them to set up a common command under Marshal Foch as Supreme Allied Commander.

By the summer a million United States troops were ready for action, the bulk of them formed into a single striking force under General Pershing. Hundreds of tanks – which the Germans lacked – had reached the front from American and British factories. Foch first drove in a number of German salients and, as the Germans withdrew, launched a general offensive, the French bearing the brunt of it in the centre, the British, led by Haig, in the north west, the Americans in the east.

Soon the Germans were in full retreat. Though their troops retired in good order to the last, there were strikes and riots at home and mutiny in the fleet. Meanwhile, Greece having entered the war, an allied force, under the French General, Franchet-Desperey, drove

How the world changed

through the Balkans from Salonika, forced Bulgaria to sue for peace at the end of September and enabled the Rumanians to plunge into Transylvania. On October 3rd the German Government asked President Wilson for peace and an exchange of notes continued. Turkey capitulated at the end of October and Austria on November 3rd. The Kaiser abdicated and fled to Holland; at 11.0 a.m. on November 11th, German plenipotentiaries accepted the Allies' terms, and the Armistice was signed at Compiègne in France.

So ended the Great War amid scenes of wild jubilation in London and the other Allied capitals. Germany had lost over two million dead, Russia at least 1,700,000, France 1,400,000, the British Empire, including India, 1,090,000, Austria-Hungary 1,200,000, Italy 460,000, the USA 115,660, Rumania and Turkey over 300,000 each, Serbia, more than half its fighting men.

Summary

In 1917 there was the same trial of strength in France and Flanders with the same dreadful casualty lists. The British General Allenby defeated the Turks and took Jerusalem.

The war at sea became fierce. The British blockade stopped Germany importing food and raw materials. On their side, the Germans stepped up their submarine campaign, sinking at sight any ships – including American ships – bound for Britain, France or Italy.

There was great weariness with the war; mutinies in France, strikes in Germany; peace proposals by the Pope, Benedict XV.

Three important things happened this year: (1) the Russian Revolution, which led to Russia being knocked out of the war; (2) the decision of the United States to come into the war against Germany; (3) the Balfour Declaration by which the British Government promised to help establish a Jewish national home in Palestine after the war.

American ships and supplies gave growing support to the Allies. The German General, Ludendorff, made a desperate attempt to break through in the west before the main body of American troops could reach France, but in vain.

In the summer the French and British, now helped by a million American troops, started to roll the Germans back. Meanwhile another Allied offensive, starting from Salonika, forced Bulgaria to sue for peace. Austria surrendered on November 3rd and Germany on November 11th, 1918. Ten million people had been killed.

Chapter 7 *The Peace Treaties and the League of Nations*

The Peace Conference opened in Paris in January, 1919, and completed its treaty-making in June 1920, leaving a good many loose ends to be tied up by a Conference of Ambassadors of the victorious powers, a Reparations Commission and the newly formed League of Nations.

The treaties were all signed in various suburbs of Paris from which they took their titles. The *Treaty of Versailles* (June 28th, 1919) ended the state of war with Germany, imposed many penalties upon it and restored to France Alsace and Lorraine, which Germany had taken in 1870. The *Treaty of Saint Germain-en-Laye* (September 10th, 1919) reduced Austria, separated from Hungary, to a small country of 80,000 square kilometres, which was forbidden to unite with Germany. The *Treaty of Neuilly* (November 27th, 1919) with Bulgaria, obliged it to cede Eastern Thrace to Greece. The *Treaty of Sèvres*, signed in the china factory (April 11th, 1920) dismembered Turkey. This was the one treaty which a defeated country at once tore up; for Kemal Ataturk raised his nation against its humiliating conditions. It was replaced by the negotiated Treaty of Lausanne (1923). Finally the *Treaty of the Trianon* (June 4th, 1920) cut down Hungary to a landlocked country of 90,000 square kilometres, in the Danubian plain, giving about two thirds of its former territories to Rumania and to the newly created Jugo-Slavia and Czechoslovakia. There remained a treaty to recognize the restored Poland, once its frontiers were determined, and sixteen treaties, declarations and conventions guaranteeing the rights of racial, religious and linguistic minorities in the various

41

national states into which Central and Eastern Europe were divided.

This was meant to be a permanent Peace Settlement. How was it that in twenty years it was in ruins?

First of all, the wishes of the peoples who had won the war were very different from one another. In Britain the first feeling was one of heart-felt relief and a wish to get back to the normal life of peace, which had been so cruelly disturbed four years before. 'Keep the home fires burning till the boys come home', had been a popular song. But for those who did come home, home turned out to be a very different place from the familiar picture of it. Jobs were not easy to find. To the artificial prosperity of war-time there succeeded a state of affairs in which exports fell to less than half what they were in 1914; and by 1920 there were already 1,200,000 unemployed. So bitter resentment against Germany followed the short period of rejoicing at the coming of peace. The popular newspapers turned this into strident cries of 'Hang the Kaiser!' and 'Squeeze Germany until the pips squeak'. 370 Members of Parliament, elected in the 'Khaki' election, sent a telegram to Mr Lloyd George at the Peace Conference, demanding that Germany should be made to pay in full.

Monsieur Clémenceau, the tough old French Premier, certainly voiced the feelings of most Frenchmen in demanding punishment, guarantees against any future aggression from Germany, which had invaded France twice in a life-time, and payment for the vast amount of damage done. A great band of devastation stretched right across the country from the North Sea to the Swiss frontier, as well as through Belgian Flanders. 10,000 factories were out of action. The coal mines of the Nord and the Pas-de-Calais were so damaged that in the first year of peace they produced only two million tons of coal as against the normal eighteen million. There was no unemployment, because so many men had been killed (1,400,000) and gravely wounded (600,000), that the work of reconstruction absorbed all available labour. M. Clémenceau had very little use for the higher thoughts of President Wilson and others.

In the United States there was a very different mood. There was no demand for reparations. There was pride in the victorious achievement of the American army (it was not long before school history books were giving the impression that it won the war single-handed). The idea of breaking up the empires appealed to the traditional anti-imperial feelings of the Americans, and the President's idea of building a new world on the basis of national freedom and democracy was popular, particularly with his Democratic Party. Production both of industry and agriculture had been immensely expanded by the war and its end brought no reduction in Europe's demand for American goods – for the first two years at least. On the other hand there was a strong feeling that the war had been only a temporary exception to the rule, that the United States should not be entangled in the Old World's affairs. The Republican Party, which obtained a majority in Congress in 1919 against President Wilson's Democratic Party, soon carried most of the people with it in deciding to return to isolation.

This gives some idea of the climate in which three men, Wilson, Clémenceau and Lloyd George, and their delegations, had to produce the Peace Treaties. For it was they who were really decisive. Orlando, the Italian, who formed with them the 'Big Four', got little attention. The lesser powers on the winning side, of course, staked their claims, especially Poland and the countries carved out of Austria and Hungary. Russia, in which civil war was raging, was left out of the picture.

But none of the defeated governments were allowed to take part in the Peace Conference or in framing the Treaties. This was a fatal mistake. The Peace, unlike that negotiated by every previous European Conference, was an imposed peace. From the first the Germans were able to say that the Treaty, which they were compelled to sign at Versailles, was a *Diktat*. Hungarians, Austrians, Turks and Bulgarians felt the same. This meant that from the start patriotism in every defeated country was bitterly against the Treaty. Therefore it was only so long as the victors were united in their policies that they could hope to maintain the terms which they had imposed. This applied particularly to the restrictions put upon Germany, such as the allied occupation and demilitarization of the Rhineland, the transfer of the Saar mines to French ownership, the huge bill for reparations (scaled down bit by

43

bit), and the almost complete disarmament (no tanks, no air force, practically no navy, and an army limited to 100,000).

The League of Nations

The Covenant of the League of Nations represented a real desire to create a means of settling disputes without war, altering treaties by consent and promoting international disarmament and co-operation in every field. This was President Wilson's main interest. It was worked out by a Commission of the Peace Conference, on which the British delegate was Lord Robert Cecil. President Wilson himself and the South African, General Smuts, played leading parts. But, though all the defeated powers were excluded from the League for several years, the Covenant formed Part I of each of the Treaties, which they had to sign.

The victorious alliance soon fell apart. First of all – and this was a fatal blow to the League – the Congress of the United States refused in March 1920 to ratify the Treaties and with them the Covenant. The withdrawal of the Americans caused the collapse of an Anglo-American Treaty of Guarantee of France against German aggression, which had only been signed in June 28th, 1919. This made the French more than ever determined to secure reparations and provide for their own security. That was why the Ruhr – the great coal-mining area of Germany – was occupied by French and Belgian troops in January 1923. France also quickly constructed a system of alliances with the new states of Central Europe – Poland, Czechoslovakia, Yugoslavia and Rumania – who were anxious to retain the territories which they had gained at the expense of Germany, Austria, Hungary and Russia. British opinion, however, drifted further and further away from the French. After a few months, British, like American, economists and bankers were much more interested in enabling Germany to recover from the chaos of defeat and play its former part in the trade and industry of Europe, than in the penal clauses of the Treaty.

Six years after the Great War, passions having cooled and economic life having become more normal, there started a period of reconcilia-

44

tion. Mr Briand and Herr Stresemann, the French and German Foreign Ministers, and Sir Austin Chamberlain, the British Foreign Secretary, were the principal architects of it. The Agreements made in October 1925 at Locarno provided a mutual guarantee of the frontiers between Germany, France and Belgium. In 1926 Germany was admitted to the League of Nations. In 1928 Briand succeeded in persuading the United States to peep our of its isolation, and the Briand-Kellogg Pact to 'outlaw war as an instrument of national policy' was signed on behalf of sixty governments in Paris. At the end of 1929 the British evacuated their zone of occupation in the Rhineland, and the French and Belgian troops withdrew soon after.

1925 - 1930 was the period in which the League of Nations seemed to become a real influence in world affairs. Foreign Ministers of the European powers attended its Assemblies; Germany took its place with France, the British Empire, Italy and Japan as a permanent member of its Council. Special departments of the League had proved their worth. The International Labour Organization had already negotiated an impressive number of conventions to protect the interests of the workers. The Permanent Mandates Commission had established an effective way of supervising the administration by the Allies of the colonial territories which they had taken from Germany and of former Turkish provinces. The authority of the Permanent Court of International Justice was strengthened; by 1929 forty-two countries, including Britain, had accepted its 'compulsory jurisdiction' in all questions of international law. It seemed therefore possible to attempt the most difficult task of all, that of making a general disarmament treaty.

We shall see as we go on with the story how these high hopes came to be dashed; how the League completely failed to stop the revival of Japanese, German and Italian militarism; and how in the late 'thirties a new world war became inevitable. The main reasons were the *disunion* of the democratic powers – the USA, Britain and France; and even more, that very desire for peace and quiet, which was the most abiding popular reaction from the First World War. The failure of France and Britain in March 1936 to stop Hitler occupying the

How the world changed

Rhineland with German troops, in violation of the Peace Treaty, showed him and the world that they would never meet him, until it was too late, with the only argument which the militarist can understand; which is force.

Summary

The Peace Conference of the victorious Allies met in Paris in January 1919 and made separate Peace Treaties with Germany (Treaty of Versailles), Austria, Hungary, Bulgaria and Turkey; a treaty to recognize Poland, now independent; and many special treaties to safeguard minorities, etc.

By the Versailles Treaty the Germans were obliged to restore Alsace-Lorraine to France and to transfer the part of Poland which they had governed; to pay an indefinite amount of reparations; to hand over their mines in the Saar to the French and to reduce their forces to a maximum of 100,000 men. The West Bank of the Rhine was to be occupied by French and British Broops.

The Treaties with Austria and Hungary broke up those countries into a number of national states.

The Covenant of the new League of Nations was made Part I of each of the Peace Treaties. All these treaties were *imposed* on the defeated nations; they were not allowed to take any part in framing them. That is why it was easy to arouse patriotic feeling in Germany and the other countries against these dictated treaties.

It was only so long as the victorious powers were united that they could enforce them. But the United States Senate refused to ratify the Treaties, including the Covenant. America's absence weakened the League from the first and very soon the British and French governments drifted apart.

In spite of this the League established itself and organized much international cooperation. Germany, France and Britain were reconciled in 1925 by the Locarno Treaty. Then for four or five years the League became the meeting place of the Foreign Ministers and seemed to have a real influence in world affairs. It collapsed when faced with the challenge of Japanese, German and Italian militarism in the 1930s.

Part 3 1919 - 1939
The uneasy peace

Chapter 8 *The new map of Europe*

If we compare the map on page 48 with the one on page 10, we can see the many changes resulting from the Great War.

Germany had to give up Bismarck's conquests – Schleswig to Denmark and Alsace-Lorraine, with its iron ore, to France, as well as Pomerania and a great deal of Upper Silesia, with its coal mines, to Poland. Italy took from Austria the Trentino and the South Tyrol with its German-speaking people – a cause of trouble ever since – as well as Trieste, which had been the chief seaport of Austria.

But the most dramatic change in Central and Eastern Europe was that, instead of the whole area being governed by two great Empires, the Austrian and the Russian, it was now split into eight small states and parts of two more. The Austrian Empire, ruled for centuries by the Habsburg monarchy, was a great 'common market' providing freedom of communications and trade from the Ukraine to the Adriatic and from Germany to the Balkans, and it had long been a buffer between the two great rivals for power, Russia and Germany. None of the small countries into which it was now split up was strong enough on its own to stop the expansion of either of these two ambitious neighbours. Consequently within twenty years Nazi Germany had overrun and subdued all of them, and in another five years Communist Russia had, in its turn, invaded and brought all of them under its control. If it had been possible to convert this great Empire into a commonwealth or federation, in which the various national groups had equal rights, the history of Europe would have been very

different. But things had gone too far to save it, owing to the national feelings which the war brought to the boil.

Borderlands of Russia

Let us trace these changes on the map of Europe from north to south. There was no change in the frontiers of Norway and Sweden which were neutral in the war. Finland had secured independence, for which its people had long struggled, from Russia. So had Esthonia, Latvia and Lithuania, whose peoples, like the Finns, were quite different from the Russians in race and religion. Poland, which had been 'partitioned' between Russia, Austria and Germany, was restored as an independent Republic. Having driven back the Red Army which nearly took Warsaw in 1920, the Poles pushed their frontier far to the east, so as to take in a lot of the Ukraine and White Russia.

The 'successor states'

Next we come to the long, artificial state of Czechoslovakia. It was made up of Bohemia and Moravia, in which the Czechs predominated, and which had been Austrian, and of Slovakia and Ruthenia, which had been part of Hungary. Prague was the new capital. While all these people were of Slav origin, the Czechs formed the ruling group from the first, while the Ruthenians were of the same nation and religious rite as the Ukrainians of Galicia. Austria and Hungary were now entirely independent of one another. Austria was struggling to keep alive with a quarter of its population in the old imperial capital of Vienna. Hungary was flooded with refugees from the territories which it had lost, and was torn with civil war. Soon after the defeat, Bela Kun had established a Communist Government; this gave the Rumanian army the pretext to occupy Budapest and loot it to their hearts' content. Once they were withdrawn under Allied pressure, a counter-revolution, led by Admiral Horthy, took over.

Rumania had more than doubled its territory thanks to its being on the winning side in the last days of the war. It took Bessarabia, the rich corn-growing province between the Rivers Dnieper and Pruth, from Russia, and the whole of Transylvania, together with part of the fertile Banat in the South, from Hungary. The wooded and mountainous province of Transylvania, rich in ores, had been part of the Hungarian Kingdom for 900 years, but a majority of the peasantry there were Rumanian. They had been the underlings, like the Irish countryfolk had been under English landlords in Ireland. They now took their revenge.

Jugoslavia, or the land of the South Slavs, which was called in the peace treaty 'the Kingdom of the Serbs, Croats and Slovenes', was the third large 'successor state'. Here the Serbs were the dominant partners. The Serbs first compelled the old kingdom of Montenegro to join Serbia (by the simple method of training machine guns on the Montenegrin delegation) and then founded a new composite state, with Croatia and part of the Banat taken from Hungary, and with Slovenia, Bosnia and Herzogovina taken from Austria.

The attempt to protect minorities

All these dismemberments of the old Empires were justified on the principle of 'national self-determination' of which President Wilson was the champion. But the population of Central Europe had been built up as the result of migration, conquest, settlement and trade through the centuries, long before the 'principle of nationality' became all the rage. Consequently, within the frontiers of the newly formed and enlarged states, there were large numbers of people of different national origin from their new rulers. Of these new 'racial, religious and linguistic minorities', as they were now called, there were in Poland three million Ruthenians (Catholics of the Eastern rite) who had been under Austria, a million White Russian (Orthodox), half a million Germans, and the Lithuanian population of Vilna which the Poles had seized. Czechoslovakia had three and a half million Austrian Germans in the Sudetenland and nearly a million Hungarians. In Jugoslavia twelve out of thirteen million were of the various South Slav peoples which we have mentioned, the remaining million mainly Hungarian. In Rumania thirty per cent of the population were of different national and religious minorities, the Hungarians forming the largest group, then the Germans, Jews, Ruthenians, Russians, Bulgars and Turks.

In the hope of preventing oppression and reducing friction the principal Allies insisted on Poland and the 'successor states' signing Minorities Treaties, and these were placed under the guarantee of the Council of the League of Nations. That guarantee turned out to be almost entirely worthless, chiefly owing to the intrigues of the governments concerned and the indifference of the Great Powers. But the treaties themselves were not worthless, because they obliged each of these countries to make laws providing for equal rights for all their citizens, whatever their race, language or creed. Though there were many injustices, especially in the early days, this meant that the Courts were obliged to deal with cases in which a breach of these laws was alleged. In Czechoslovakia at least this legal protection of minorities worked honestly.

The Council of the League had to rule the Saar district, where the French operated the mines, and to arrange a plebiscite to decide its future after fifteen years. To ensure that this was done fairly, the League organized the first international peace-keeping force in history to supervise it in 1935. This resulted in the return of the district to Germany.

The real power of nationality

We shall see in later chapters what happend to the countries which the Peace Conference of Paris put on the map. The Baltic States have been swallowed by the USSR and other changes made on the Soviet borders. But the other national states as they were formed at this time have managed for the most part to keep their national character and their frontiers, whether under Nazi or Communist control This shows that, for all the mistakes made in the Peace Settlement of 1919-1920, there was a genuine basis for the changes made in the name of 'national self-determination'. It is because of this that we can see a marked increase of national independence in the Communist-ruled countries of Eastern Europe today.

How the world changed

Summary

The changes in the map of Europe caused by the War nearly all resulted from making new national states, or enlarging others which were on the winning side. This was done by taking land from the defeated Austrian and German Empires and from Russia, weakened by Revolution.

Germany had to give up some old conquests to France, Denmark and Poland. Italy took some German-speaking areas from Austria – which has caused trouble ever since.

Russia lost *Finland, Estonia, Latvia* and *Lithuania*. *Poland* was restored as an independent country and conquered also much of the Ukraine and White Russia.

The Empire of Austria-Hungary was split up. It had been ruled for centuries by the Habsburg monarchy. It had formed a great 'common market' and a buffer between the two ambitious rivals, Germany and Russia. None of the small countries into which it was divided was strong enough to resist either of them.

Poland took Galicia from Austria. The new *Czechoslovakia* was made up of territory taken from Austria and Hungary. *Rumania* more than doubled its territory, chiefly at the expense of Hungary, and took Bessarabia from Russia. *Yugoslavia* was formed by taking the Slav peoples from Austria and Hungary and adding them to Serbia and Montenegro.

Minorities Treaties were drawn up to safeguard the rights of racial and religious minorities in these 'successor states'. They did not have much effect.

The national character of the people in most of these states has survived, even under their present Communist governments.

Chapter 9 *The Russian Revolution and the Soviet Union*

The Russian Revolution had two causes. One was the misery of the people, especially in the towns; the other was the small group of well-organized revolutionaries, driven underground or abroad, whose

52

plans to take advantage of this situation were well prepared in advance. There were only four and a half million industrial workers out of a population of 140 million, but they formed a 'proletariat', easy to lead. Four fifths of the population were peasants, mostly living in village communes. There was little desire in the countryside for violent change, but, as everywhere, the peasants wanted to own land of their own. There were some six million independent farmers: most of the others worked as tenants of landowners or of the Crown. Serious attempts had been made during the last twenty years to improve conditions of country life, as, for instance, through the educational work of liberal gentry and professional people in the 'Back to the village' movement. But conditions of life for the majority were very low, and the war had increased poverty and discontent everywhere. Inflation had more than doubled the price of bread. The hardships of the soldiers, mostly peasants, had become intolerable. Ill-led and equipped they had been thrown into badly organized offensives, causing appalling losses. The Czar, a weak man, surrounded by intriguers, no longer inspired loyalty as 'the Little Father' of his people.

The Revolution of March 1917

The shortage of food produced riots and a general transport strike in Petrograd[1] at the beginning of 1917. On March 12th the soldiers of the garrison, themselves raw recruits, mutinied and refused to move against the crowd; and without the army, government collapsed. The parliament (the Duma) refused to be dismissed by the Czar and formed a Provisional Government, mostly of Liberal and Socialist members, under Prince Lvov, with Kerensky, who became Minister of War, as his chief assistant. The Czar abdicated. The aim was to transform Russia into a democratic republic and to continue the war. But the people were sick of war.

In April the German General Staff smuggled Lenin, the leader of the exiled Russian revolutionaries, and other active Bolsheviks,[2] who

[1] Then called St Petersburg, now Leningrad.
[2] *Bolsheviks* means those who were in the *majority* at a meeting of the Russian Socialist Party in London in 1903, while the *Mensheviks* were the *minority* who opposed the use of violence.

now took the name of Communists, in a sealed railway waggon from neutral Switzerland into Russia. Their object was to destroy the military power of Russia from inside; and so they did, in the short run. They little knew that under Lenin's leadership the Russian Empire, instead of breaking up in disorder, would become a great socialist state, which in less than a lifetime would join in crushing Germany.

The Bolshevik Revolution of October 1917

A 'Soviet (Council) of Workers and Peasants' had been formed in Petrograd, and very quickly – owing particularly to the help of the railwaymen – soviets were established in Moscow and many other towns and among the deserting soldiers.

The Petrograd Soviet supported the Provisional Government, but Lenin, a great mob-orator, set to work to undermine it. In July, after the disastrous failure of Kerensky's offensive against the Austrians, the Bolsheviks, now 200,000 strong, attempted to seize power: they failed and Lenin fled to Finland. Kerensky, however, was threatened in September by General Kornilov and his army marching on Petrograd to oppose the Soviet: he appealed to the workers to defend the city. This was the final opportunity for the Bolsheviks. Lenin returned and led a rising against the Government. On the night of November 6th, 1917 (October 24th in the Russian Calendar), armed workers seized strategic points in Petrograd. Kerensky was arrested in the country, but escaped. Next day a 'Council of People's Commissars' was set up, with Lenin as President. That was the beginning of the Communist Government of Russia. Next month a Constituent Assembly called by the Provisional Government to frame a democratic constitution attempted to meet. But only a quarter of the elected deputies supported the Bolsheviks. Lenin therefore prevented them meeting by force. The Revolution met with growing resistance; clearly it could not succeed so long as the war continued. Trotsky, one of the Commissars, took on the task of negotiating with the Germans. An armistice was signed with them in December 1917 and a Peace Treaty at Brest Litovsk on March 3rd, 1918. By this treaty, the Bolsheviks lost a quarter of the population of the old Empire, three quarters of its iron mines and its best wheat growing land. It was a heavy price to pay.

Russia and World Revolution

In the minds of Lenin and his colleagues their Russian Revolution was meant to be only the beginning of a World Revolution. This is because their whole purpose came from accepting the explanation of *world* history invented in the nineteenth century by Karl Marx and his theory that, just as in the past one class had overthrown another for economic reasons, so at this stage the 'workers' were sure, sooner or later, to overthrow the 'capitalists'. It was the task of the communists, as professional revolutionaries, to hasten this defeat of capitalism – meaning the existing order of things as Marx knew it – and thereafter to establish a classless society. Since they were Russians, Russia had to be their starting point. So, even in the midst of the civil war, confusion and famine which followed his seizure of power, Lenin summoned a conference in Moscow (January to March 1919) to found the Communist International. Zinoviev, President of the International, wrote in the first number of its Review[1]:

> *Old Europe is dashing at mad speed towards the proletarian revolution. . . . In a year the whole of Europe will be Communist. And the struggle for Communism will be transferred to America, perhaps to Asia and to other parts of the world.*

This was a wild piece of wishful thinking. Revolutionary Councils were in fact formed among the defeated German troops at the end of 1918, but were quickly suppressed. The attempted rising in Bavaria was soon put down; and the communist regime of Bela Kun in Hungary only lasted 113 days. Almost all the trade unions outside Russia were hostile to the Revolution. It is not surprising that, with an aggressive programme like this, the new rulers of Russia made enemies of all their neighbours, as well as the victorious Allies. It was only in 1921 that the Revolution in Russia itself can be said to have triumphed,

[1] *Kommunisticheski Internatzional.* May 1st, 1919.

after defending itself against the counter-revolutionary Russian armies of Generals Denikin, Wrangel, Kolchak and Miller, and the intervention of British and French forces in the White Sea and the Black Sea. The Bolsheviks had suffered a serious defeat by the newly formed Polish Army in 1920.

The USSR

Yet the idea of confining the revolution to Russia was never admitted. And, when the time came in 1922 to give a political framework to what was in fact the bulk of the former Russian Empire, it was not, and never has since been called *Russia*. Its title was the 'Union of Socialist Soviet Republics'. It was formed as a federation of the Russian Socialist Republic with the Ukrainian, White Russian and other smaller republics in various parts of the territory (there are now fifteen Republics in the Union), and in theory the Union could become world-wide. The great quarrel of the early days was whether, for tactical reasons, Communism should first be firmly established in Russia, or whether revolution should be attempted at the same time all over the world. Trotsky, who had successfully organized the Red Army to fight the Counter-Revolutionaries, was keen on the latter idea (which led in due course to his being exiled and murdered in Mexico). Lenin, and even more Stalin who succeeded him in the leadership, were strongly in favour of consolidating the revolution in one country, namely Russia, first.

In the early days, the revolutionaries of Petrograd and Moscow were neither known nor loved by the bulk of the Russian people and hated by many. But the fact that Russia was being attacked by foreigners between 1918 and 1920 and defended by the Red Army raised the national patriotism of the majority. Once again, hatred of the Nazi invaders made the Second World War for all Russians 'the Great Patriotic War'.

Lenin

Lenin (Vladimir Oulianov was his real name) had been wholly devoted to the revolutionary cause since one of his brothers had been hanged for his part in a plot against the Czar in 1887. During his long exile he had thought out the means of adapting the theories of Marx to modern times and developed a strategy of his own. Consequently when he came to power he was a vigorous teacher of ideas, and his writings soon became a kind of Bible in forming the minds of the Russians. Marxism-Leninism is the official creed of the country. He was also a realist. In 1921, seeing that too rapid an advance to socialism would defeat its purpose, he introduced the 'New Economic Policy' (NEP). Instead of having to hand over all their grain to the state, the peasants, after paying a tax in kind, could sell the rest of their crops. While the land belonged to the state, the village commune (an old Russian institution called *mir*) kept the full use of it. Trade was made free again. Small businesses could operate without interference. Co-operatives were encouraged. The results of this easing of pressure were good. By 1924, agricultural production, which had fallen disastrously, had almost recovered its 1913 level.

Lenin died in 1924. He had been the great hero of the Revolution. His body was mummified and placed in a large tomb in front of the Kremlin in Moscow. Petrograd was named Leningrad after him.

Stalin

Joseph Djugashvili, who took the name Stalin, succeeded Lenin. He was a Georgian who, unlike the exiled Bolsheviks, had rarely left Russia. Lenin made him Commissar for Nationalities in the early days of the Revolution, and it was largely his work that caused the various non-Russian republics to take their place, with the Russians, in the Union of Socialist Soviet Republics, whose constitution was adopted as Lenin lay dying in January 1924. Through the struggles for power of the leading Communists, Stalin had worked his way up to the post of Secretary General of the Communist Party, the most powerful position in the state. Under him the Party (at that time two per cent of the adult population) with the political police which it controlled, became the means by which he forced through the economic reorganization of the country and ruthlessly crushed opposition. Trotsky was expelled from the Party in 1927 and banished in 1929: his supporters were shot or exiled.

How the world changed

The fact that the clumsy attempts at international revolution had isolated the new Russia from the rest of the world justified, and helped, Stalin in concentrating upon internal development. A series of Five-Year Plans were introduced, the first from 1928 to 1932 and the second from 1933 to 1937; the third, starting in 1938, was interrupted by the Second World War. The NEP was quickly abandoned; those who had profited by it, and particularly the more prosperous peasants or *kulaks*, were denounced as enemies of the people and killed or deported to forced labour camps. All industry was nationalized and organized in state trusts and combines.

The collectivization of agriculture started in earnest in 1929. This meant that all the peasants were ordered to work in great collective farms (*kolkozes*), combining several villages or state farms (*sovckozes*), without any land of their own. It was here that Stalin encounted fierce opposition, which was never entirely quelled, despite deportations to forced labour camps and other harsh measures. The persecution of the Orthodox Church was another great grievance of many country-folk, for the Communists were bitterly opposed to all religion. At first many peasants killed their cattle and burnt their crops rather than submit. Production fell disastrously; there was only half as much live-stock as before the Revolution. Eventually Stalin (in 1937) allowed the peasants to keep a smallholding and some beasts of their own, while working for the *kolkoz*. This, and the progress made in the mechanization of agriculture, brought the production of grain, though not of meat cattle, up to the pre-war level.

Rapid industrialization

But it was in the creation of heavy industry and of the many secondary industries, such as those making tractors and motor vehicles, and the development of power, that Stalin's policy had most success. By 1940 the production of electric power was fifteen times what it had been when the Plans started: three times as much coal was being dug, and the USSR had become the second largest producer of petrol in the world. The output of the great metallurgical industries was the largest, after that of the United States and of Germany. All this involved the founding of new industrial towns, and the exploiting of natural resources all over the territory of the Union, in Central Asia, the Volga-Ural region and in Siberia, as well as the expansion of the old towns. The price of this policy was a great shortage of consumer goods. The standard of life remained low and housing conditions were very bad.

Despotism

In the process Stalin undoubtedly became an absolute ruler and, like all despots, he was more and more suspicious of rivals. Arrests and executions multiplied, particularly among the higher ranks of the Party and government. The assassination of Kirov, a leader of the Party, in 1934 started a series of 'purges' which ended by Stalin having at least seven million people shot or deported, including nearly all his original Bolshivik colleagues, diplomats, engineers, and, most serious of all, a large number of generals and other senior officers in the Army. Russia was to know the cost of this when war came.

Changing tactics in foreign policy

The Soviet Government in its first twenty years was in no state to undertake foreign adventures. The Communist International and the national Communist parties, though duly kept at work, were really more of an embarrassment than an asset, except for the important growth of the Chinese Party. Chicherin, who succeeded Trotsky as Foreign Commissar, negotiated a treaty with Germany, the other international outcast, at Rapallo in 1922. But Stalin badly needed foreign technicians to make a success of the Five-Year Plans, and these were gradually obtained from Britain and other countries. It was the task of Litvinoff, who was Commissar of Foreign Affairs from 1930 to 1939, to cultivate the friendship of the Western Powers. The Soviet Government was admitted in 1934 to the League of Nations which they had originally called 'the Holy Alliance of the bourgeoisie for the suppression of the proletarian revolution'. In 1935 the tactics of 'the Trojan Horse' (meaning the penetration of trade unions and other groups and parties) were adopted at the 7th Congress of the Comintern, and for four years the Communist Parties, at the behest of Moscow, vigorously worked for an 'United Front against War and

How the world changed

Fascism'. This was because the Soviets feared, and with good reason, the military ambitions of Hitler's Germany in alliance with Fascist Italy, and wanted to have the support of their probable enemies. In August 1939, however, the Communists suddenly had to abandon this line of propaganda in favour of friendship with Germany, when Stalin, seeing that the French and British had abandoned Czechoslovakia to Hitler, made the fatal pact with him. The key to these changes of policy is not to be found in any principles understood by the non-Communist world. It is to be found in the determination of Stalin to protect Soviet Russia in the changing circumstances, while he was building it up as a great industrial power.

Summary

In March 1917 the Petrograd garrison mutinied. The Parliament (Duma) compelled the Czar to abdicate and formed a Provincial Government. It continued the war, which was unpopular. It summoned a Constituent Assembly to draw up a democratic constitution.

This was not at all the 'dictatorship of the proletariat' which the exiled Bolsheviks wanted. On November 6th, their leader, Lenin, succeeded in overthrowing the Provisional Government and forming a Communist government.

A peace treaty with Germany was signed in March 1918: Russia gave up its rule over Finland, the Baltic Provinces, Poland and the Ukraine. It took three years of civil war before the Revolutionary Government was in control of the rest of the Russian Empire and most of the Ukraine was recovered.

The Russian Revolution was meant to be the start of the World Revolution, and the Communist International was founded in Moscow in 1919 to promote it. But all governments and most trade unions in the world were opposed to the spread of Communism. Russia took the form of a 'Union of Socialist Soviet Republics' but, except for partial success in China, Communist power was confined to Russia till the Second World War.

Lenin, seeing the chaos caused by a too rapid advance to socialism, brought in a 'New Economic Policy' (NEP) in 1921. The peasants were allowed to sell part of their crops and trade was made free.

Lenin died in 1924. He was succeeded by Stalin. He soon became an absolute dictator, using the Communist Party and the political police to force through the economic reorganization of the country.

NEP was abolished and the farms were forced into 'collectives'. Stalin succeeded in creating heavy industries and expanding electric power in two Five-Year Plans.

In 1934 he started the great 'purges' to get rid of rivals in the Party and any suspected opponents. This ended by millions of people being shot or deported to forced labour camps. Stalin concentrated upon making Russia a great industrial power.

He had no foreign adventures. In 1934 the USSR joined the League of Nations. From then till 1939 it sought support in Britain and France because of the growing danger of German aggression. When the British and French had failed to save Czechoslovakia from the Nazis, Stalin reversed his policy and made a pact with Hitler.

Chapter 10 *Life in the Western World: Economic Crisis*

The good life

For a great many people in the Western World life was very enjoyable, especially in the ten years which followed the First World War and again in the later 1930s. The 'gay 'twenties' were not only a reaction against the sufferings and restrictions of war-time. There was a feeling of freedom and 'emancipation' among the younger generation. They felt that they must make their own future, without having to obey their elders or follow the old conventional ways of life. One no longer went to church, for instance, just because it was respectable.

Young men and girls mixed much more freely. There was much more dancing than before. It was the great age of jazz, the catching Negro-American rhythm which soon invaded Europe. Then, for the more sophisticated, there were the songs from the many good musical

How the world changed

shows of the period, like Noel Coward's *Bitter Sweet*, or the light operas of Franz Lehar.

The comforts of life to which we are accustomed today also increased very quickly during these years. Small cars, for example, were soon cheap and plentiful. In France André Citroën started the mass production of a four-seater model as early as 1919. Soon the great American firms, General Motors, Fords and Chryslers, were pouring shiploads of automobiles into Europe, and Morris began mass-producing popular models in England. There was far more moving about; the isolation of country life broke down. Doctoring became more skilful. One of the most important events in medical history was the discovery of penicillin by Sir Alexander Fleming in 1928. It saved the lives of thousands of wounded men in the next great war.

Travelling by air

The last ten years of this period marked the rapid progress of aviation towards a service of transport across the world. Colonel Lindbergh's solo flight across the Atlantic from New York to Le Bourget (Paris), where he made a night landing, witnessed by an immense crowd in 1927, was the first great 'break-through' from short-distance hops. Soon the British Imperial Airways, with their four engine flying boats, had reduced the journey to Calcutta to three days, with forty passengers. Almost all the long-distance flying until the Second World War was done by flying boats, landing in lakes (the Dead Sea for instance), or at seaports (as Brindisi, Piraeus, Alexandria). KLM, the Dutch airline, however, developed flights by ground-landing planes to Batavia in the East Indies: they, British Airways and Air France built up regular postal and passenger services within Europe. The Americans reduced the flying time from New York to Paris or London to twenty hours; and there was much public excitement about the efforts of Amy Johnson and other pioneers to reduce the time of air flights to Australia.

Civilization becoming uniform

For various reasons more and more people moved into the great towns, so that Western civilization came to be an *urban* civilization.

For instance, in Britain eighty-three per cent of the population was living in cities of over 100,000 in 1939 as against seventy-five per cent in 1914, and the population of London had increased by 1,700,000. Berlin had increased by over a million in the same period. It was also becoming a *uniform* civilization. Not only was this due to the mass production in the factories of the United States, Britain and Western Europe of many of the necessities and accessories of life, but popular information and entertainment was also becoming very much the same everywhere.

The extraordinary development of the American cinema industry was one reason for this. A day after Charlie Chaplin's film *The Gold Rush* appeared in London in 1925, one saw in Paris great posters of *La Ruée vers l'Or*, and next day in Rome placards of *Il Corso del Oro*. (That was something quite new then; it is commonplace today.) Newsreels also, giving much the same news in every country, were in each cinema programme.

The attraction of the cinema was greatly increased by the introduction of sound films, instead of the old silent films with captions. First shown in the USA in 1928, they were destined to supply much of the material for television which, though started by the BBC in the late 1930s, was held up by the outbreak of war. Meanwhile 'the wireless' with its news, music and plays was firmly established in the majority of homes. Walt Disney's first animated cartoons began with Mickey Mouse in 1925.

It was in these same years that the huge football and sports stadiums were built and the Olympic Games became of world-wide importance. But, unfortunately, neither international sport, nor the fact that most people in America and Europe now had the same news, the same entertainments and the same habits, made for peace. The governments in most countries – though not Britain or America – soon took control of the broadcasting stations and used them for their own national propaganda; and the sports stadiums of Germany and Italy became the favourite setting for huge Nazi and Fascist military parades.

How the world changed

Economics

Not only the wealthy, but most people having a regular occupation, could lead a fairly comfortable life and amuse themselves in these inter-war years – even in Germany when the catastrophe of defeat and the following inflation had been overcome. It was very different for a large number of the industrial workers and their families. Conditions varied; but it is true to say that *unemployment*, or at least chronic uncertainty of employment, was the curse of the Western industrial countries during those twenty years. One of the main reasons for this evil was that there was no international machinery – as there is today – to regulate world finance and help to maintain stability.

Britain's economic illness

Britain's economy took a long time to recover from the war. One reason for this was that wages had been raised during the war, especially in the heavy industries (coal, steel, armaments) much higher than in other European countries, and the trade unions naturally fought to keep what they had gained. Another reason was that so many of our factories were old-fashioned, so that they could not well compete with the industries which grew up in the war-damaged countries, let alone America. Another was that coal, on which Britain's prosperity had been built, was no longer the only source of industrial energy. Petrol and electricity were already serious competitors, and many of our coal mines had become unprofitable. Another reason was that we had lost a lot of our overseas markets during the war. Also the country's 'invisible exports', such as insurance and interest on British investments abroad, had gone down. The government had huge loans to repay to the United States.

The result of all this was that the prices of our goods were too high to compete in foreign markets, so that our export trade fell by 1921 to only forty-nine per cent of what it had been before the war.

This itself caused unemployment such as the country had never known before. The *dole* as it was called, that is relief for those out of work (resulting from compulsory insurance payments by employers and workers) was first introduced in 1920, but soon a great deal more

64

assistance had to be paid by the state. By 1921 there were two and a half million people unemployed. This total was halved in 1924, rose again to over one and a half million in 1926, the year of the general strike – and that of the coal miners which lasted for seven months – and to over two million again in 1930. When the great world depression hit the country, the total rose to three million. Matters were made worse by fixing the rate of exchange for the pound much too high when Britain, like many other countries, adopted once more the 'gold standard'[1] in 1926.

Only after 1931, when the pound was 'devalued' and allowed to find its true rate in international exchange, did the economy begin to pick up. Then came taxes on imports and the system of *Imperial Preferences*, adopted at the Ottawa Conference of 1932, by which imports and exports between Britain and the Dominions were given reduced tariffs. Many new industries (like those making motor cars, aircraft, electrical appliances, household goods, etc.) were developed. In the late 1930s rearmament also helped. This made a great improvement; the number of unemployed went down steadily and the general standard of living was much higher by the outbreak of the Second World War, though there was always a 'hard core' of about 500,000 people out of work.

The memory of unemployment

This sad story shows why the memory of the massive unemployment between 1919 and 1932 burnt itself into the soul of the British Labour Party and the trade union movement. It had brought dreadful unhappiness, most of all to the families of the miners, and those working in the heavy industries of the North and the Midlands and in shipbuilding. Mothers found it almost impossible to feed their children decently, with their husbands on the 'dole'. No wonder the demand for 'full employment' headed the list of all social policies after the Second World War.

[1] This means that the value of a country's money is officially fixed at its worth in gold – like the American dollar today, which is legally worth $\frac{1}{35}$ oz of fine gold – and can be *exchanged* for gold. The system depends upon the country's Central Bank owning a sufficient reserve of gold.

How the world changed

The Great Depression

This happened between 1929 and 1934 and was the worst financial disorder that the 'capitalist' or non-communist world has ever known. Three of its main results were: 1 a great increase in the responsibilities of the Federal government in the United States for the welfare of the whole people; 2 the rise to power of Hitler's National Socialists in Germany; 3 the creation of a new world financial system, after the Second World War, so as to prevent it ever happening again.

The United States. The Wall Street Crash

In the years after the First World War prosperity increased in the United States by leaps and bounds. Great fortunes were made and American capital was invested all over the world. In 1929 the United States accounted for 44.8 per cent of the industrial production of the whole world and had invested 5,000 million dollars in Europe, especially in Germany, where American money had both financed the Reparations payments and helped to build up new industries. But all this tremendous expansion had little to do with the government; it was the achievement of private business firms, in competition or union with one another, and very often depending on credit, i.e. money lent by banks because of what seemed to be good prospects of profit. There was more and more speculation in the buying and selling of shares. In four years (1925 - 1929) the value of shares quoted on Wall Street, the Stock Exchange of New York, had risen *twice* as much as the real value of industrial production. And the worst of it was that there was *over-production* anyway – hundreds of thousands more cars than could be sold and a glut of wheat which the farmers could not sell; and so on.

Suddenly this pack of cards came tumbling down. In October 1929 the wholesale prices of iron, steel, copper and manufactured goods started to fall. Soon panic set in on Wall Street. Share-holders, large and small, sold out their shares as quickly as they could. Nobody wanted to buy. This collapse of confidence continued, with short periods of relief, till 1934. Dozens of millionaires were ruined.

66

The Chaos Spreads

Because so much American investment was involved in Europe, disaster soon followed when American banks and financiers started pulling out their funds and stopping their loans. The dramatic political result of the bankruptcy of Austrian and German banks was one consequence of this. Britain also suffered because, owing about £400 million, mostly to the United States, it could not recover what Central European countries owed to London. This was one of the reasons for the devaluation of the pound in 1931, which immediately caused the fall of other national currencies linked to it, such as those in Scandinavia, Portugal, Egypt and South America. Hardly a single country, except the USSR, escaped.

Social consequences in the USA

In the United States, the richest country in the world, poverty and misery resulted on a huge scale – seventeen million industrial workers unemployed and fifteen million farmers ruined, through the fall of wholesale prices for their crops and lack of money to pay their bank-loans. Though each state was jealous of its rights and private property was considered sacred, there began to be a popular demand for the Federal government itself to step in and solve the crisis. In the presidential election of 1932 the Republican, President Hoover, was soundly defeated and the Democrat, Franklin Delano Roosevelt, elected with a majority of seven million votes. He campaigned firmly in favour of the rights of labour and the little man.

Roosevelt's New Deal

So soon as he succeeded, in March 1933, President Roosevelt closed all the banks, requisitioned all gold, devalued the dollar – so increasing the official gold reserves – and started upon enormous public works, at the Federal government's expense, such as roads, schools, housing projects, and, most important of all, the Tennessee Valley Authority. This operated a most ambitious complex of dams, irrigation, navigation and new industries in what had been a backward region. This

How the world changed

'New Deal' as it was called had two main sides, the *Agricultural Adjustment Act* with its low-interest credit and subsidies to farmers, and the *National Industrial Recovery Act*, which aimed at establishing good industrial relations with fair prices and a guaranteed minimum wage for the workers. Though such measures were only partially successful until the approach of war brought rearmament, the New Deal put new heart into the country. It made the Federal government much more powerful. The centre of gravity shifted from Wall Street to the White House, the President's palace, in Washington; and there it has been ever since.

A present for Adolf Hitler

The Wall Street crash had disastrous consequences in Germany. First, a great Viennese bank, the *Kredit Anstalt*, went bankrupt, ruining many people in Austria. Then the German *mark* began to fall as gold and foreign capital were withdrawn. In July 1931 one of the largest German banks, the *Danat Bank*, failed, and this set going a chain of bankruptcies. People's savings became worthless; factories closed; shopkeepers and farmers were ruined. The number of unemployed rose from one and a half million in 1929 to six million in 1931.

It was on the foundation of this widespread popular misery and discontent that the National Socialists, led by Adolf Hitler, rose to power. They promised a radical remedy to all these ills, and their propaganda turned popular discontent against the Democracies, the Communists, and especially the Jews as scapegoats for the woes of the German people. In 1928 the Nazis won only 2.3 per cent of the votes in the general election, but in 1930 they won 18.3 per cent – 6,400,000 votes – with 107 seats in the *Reichstag* (Parliament). Hitler was well on his way to supreme power.[1]

Summary

Many people in the Western world had a good time in the 1920s and the later 1930s. The younger generation felt 'emancipated'. It was the great

[1] See Chapter 12.

age of jazz and the cinema. Mass-produced motors enabled millions to move around.

Air travel began to be organized. Many advances were made in science, especially medicine. More and more people moved into great cities.

But for the working class in industrial countries the curse of the period was unemployment. Britain took twenty-five years to recover the pre-war level of her export trade.

In 1929 there was a 'crash' (collapse of confidence) on the New York stock exchange. This caused a world-wide depression, because so many countries relied on American investments; and there was no international machinery to stabilize finance and trade.

American companies and banks started to pull in their capital from Europe and stop their loans. This caused Austrian and German banks to go bankrupt; the ruin and unemployment which followed helped Hitler to gain many votes and rise to power.

Britain suffered too, with three million unemployed. In 1931 the pound was devalued, and, with the help of Imperial Preference and import tariffs, a steady recovery began.

In the USA there were seventeen million industrial unemployed and fifteen million ruined farmers. President Roosevelt (elected in 1932) pulled things together and obtained greater powers for the Federal government. He introduced the 'New Deal', with guaranteed wages for labour and subsidies for the farmers, and started great public works for economic development.

It was to prevent such a disaster happening again that the Western governments set up the International Monetary Fund and the World Bank towards the end of the Second World War.

Chapter 11 *The British Empire and Commonwealth*

Wider still and wider may thy bounds be set
God who made thee mighty, make thee mightier yet.

So ends that rousing song of A. C. Benson, 'Land of Hope and Glory', which thousands of youngsters have shouted year after year at the last night of the 'Proms',[1] though the British Empire which it was written to glorify has gone with the wind. It dates from the days soon after the First World War; it is said that it was only under pressure from King George V that Edward Elgar agreed to write the music for it.

The Empire after the victory of 1918 seemed to be at the height of its power and the old King believed fervently that it would endure. He founded then the Order of the British Empire, which continues to grow in numbers with each Honours List as a monument to that belief. There was a great Empire Exhibition at Wembley. Empire Day, which had been started to celebrate Queen Victoria's birthday (May 24th) and officially recognized since 1902, was revived in the schools of Britain and many parts of the Empire, 'as a means of training school children in good citizenship'.

It was between the wars that this simple notion of an Empire, united in loyalty to the English Crown began to weaken and to be replaced with the phrase 'The British Commonwealth and Empire', meaning a combination of the self-governing members and the colonies and protectorates etc., ruled directly from London. But nobody foresaw the complete break-up of the Empire and the disappearance of the name 'British' from the Commonwealth, which so soon followed the Second World War.

The Mandates

In 1919 the Empire comprised all those countries which we mentioned in Chapter 2, with the addition of the bulk of the territories taken from defeated Germany and Turkey. These were not, however, (except for practical purposes) strictly parts of the Empire. They were ruled under Mandates, namely authority to administer the territory, approved by the League of Nations for the good of their inhabitants, until such time as they might be able to stand on their own feet. France, Belgium, Italy, Japan and the USA also had their mandated

---

[1] The annual Promenade Concerts held in the Queen's Hall, London, till it was destroyed by a bomb in the Second World War, then in the Albert Hall.

territories. So the colonial powers were to act as trustees 'to promote to the utmost the material and moral well-being and social progress of the native peoples', with self-government as the end of the process in these territories. This principle was written into the League Covenant thanks to the South African statesman, General Smuts. It proved to be a powerful influence in moulding the future course of history. For why should it apply only to *certain* peoples in Asia, Africa and Australasia, who had passed from the control of one imperial power to that of another, and not to *all* colonies? The mandate system therefore undoubtedly sowed the seed of that general 'decolonization' which we shall describe in the second volume of this book.

The British Empire's Mandates were as follows. *The United Kingdom* had the Arab countries of Iraq, Transjordania and Palestine, detached from Turkey; and in Africa, Tanganyika – the former German East Africa – and parts of the Cameroons and Togoland. *South Africa* had the former German South-West Africa, *Australia* had part of New Guinea and *New Zealand* had Samoa. These countries were in very different stages of development and the Mandates were classified as 'A', 'B' and 'C'. 'A' Mandates were former Turkish territories with ancient civilizations of their own, which were due to become independent first. 'C' Mandates covered Papuans and South Sea islanders living in the Stone Age.

Beginning of the Commonwealth

The idea of the British Empire being transformed into a union of independent countries developed gradually. The first official expression of it resulted from the Imperial Conference of 1926, which adopted Lord Balfour's definition of the countries represented as:

> *autonomous communities within the British Empire, equal in status, in no way subordinate to one another in any aspect of their domestic or external foreign affairs, though united by a common allegiance to the Crown and freely associated as members of the British Commonwealth of Nations.*

71

How the world changed

The force of law was given to this formula in the Statute of Westminster (December 1931). The 'autonomous communities' were commonly called Dominions, though this was really only the proper title of Canada. The Statute was approved by the Parliaments of the United Kingdom, Canada, Australia, the South African Union, Newfoundland[1], the Irish Free State, and – long afterwards – New Zealand. Canada, Australia and New Zealand had almost complete self-government at the beginning of the century and the South African Union in 1909. What gave them *international* status was the fact that, having fought in the First World War, they signed the Peace Treaties and joined the League of Nations as separate states. So also did India, though the Government of India was not politically independent of London. It was, however, quite independent financially, meeting, for instance, all the cost of the Indian Army and administration from its own revenues. The Irish Free State became a member of the League in 1922.

Economics of the Commonwealth

Neither the Commonwealth as a whole nor the Colonial Empire of the United Kingdom itself was ever a 'common market' or customs union. Each colony, like each of the self-governing countries, had its own budget, tariffs and taxes.

Small colonies, like British Somaliland, often found it difficult to make both ends meet, having to pay interest on any money which they borrowed from banks or the British Treasury, though fortunate dependencies like the Malay States, who produced quantities of rubber for the tyres of the ever-increasing thousands of motor cars, became rich quickly.

It was convenient to have the resources of the Bank of England and of the City of London to fall back upon, but the Indian *rupee*, the Canadian *dollar*, and the Australian *pound*, for instance, were quite independent currencies, backed by their own reserves. Then for purposes of defence, there was the shield of the Royal Navy. These,

[1] Newfoundland became bankrupt, and was administered by the United Kingdom in the late 1930s; it became a Province of Canada in 1949.

sentiment apart, were the few material advantages of belonging to the British Empire until 1932.

In that year the Imperial Preferences adopted at the Ottawa Conference made the Commonwealth and Empire for the first time a kind of association for mutual economic benefit. For the reduction of duties – as against those charged on foreign goods – meant that food and raw materials could be imported cheaper by Britain from Australia, New Zealand, Canada, West Africa, etc., while manufactured goods from the British Isles or Canada could be imported more cheaply in return.

The old Colonial Conferences, which had become Imperial Conferences, came in the 1930s to be called 'Commonwealth Prime Ministers' Conferences'. They only met irregularly as the need arose. But a good system of consultation and exchange of information between the independent Commonwealth countries was built up through the High Commissioners, whom they kept in one another's capitals, and a Committee of Imperial Defence lasted until after the Second World War.

Decline of Imperial Power: Ireland

The first important reduction of British imperial power came with the Anglo-Irish Treaty of 1921. For the first time since Ireland was brought under the English Crown in the twelfth century, England recognized the independence of the greater part of the country.

This was the culmination of a bitter struggle. In 1916 a rising in Dublin was put down and many of the leaders shot. In December 1918 there was a general election; but the Irish Members, instead of coming to Westminster, formed a national Parliament in Dublin (*Dail Eirean*) and proclaimed the independence of Ireland, in accordance with President Wilson's principle of national self-determination. Then, for nearly three years, there was guerrilla fighting all over the country, with ambushes and assassinations by the 'Irish Republican Army', and fierce reprisals by forces of the Crown, including a tough volunteer force called the 'Black and Tans'. The sympathy of millions of Irish in America and the Dominions with the nationalist cause

73

How the world changed

added to the worries of the British government, and the war became hateful to many British as well as Irish people. Eventually Lloyd George's Government negotiated a settlement, largely through the good feeling established between Winston Churchill and one of the Irish leaders, Michael Collins.

By this settlement the Protestants of the six northern counties, who wanted to keep within the United Kingdom, were enabled to set up a Parliament of their own at Belfast, while the rest of Ireland became the Irish Free State. This was an independent Dominion within the Commonwealth. Bit by bit the legal ties between Ireland, Britain and other Commonwealth countries (like the oath of allegiance to the Crown) were loosened, till in April 1949 they were severed altogether and the Free State became the Irish Republic. Since then there has been a steady growth of understanding between the English and Irish peoples.

The attainment of Irish independence was an encouragement to the leaders of every other nationality who wanted freedom from imperial rule; it had an immediate influence upon Indian Congress leaders.

Iraq independent

The next grant of independence was to Iraq, the largest of the Arab countries. In 1930 a treaty of alliance was made with King Feisal of Iraq and two years later the Mandate was given up. This had repercussions throughout the Middle East, since all the Arab lands had been promised their independence when their leaders had been encouraged by the British to rise against the Turks. Part of the British mandated area east of the Jordan had been made an independent Emirate and then Kingdom under King Abdullah. But in the rest of Palestine the British were caught between an increasing wave of Jewish immigrants, in view of the Jewish national home which they had been promised, and the Arab majority clamouring for an independent Arab Palestine. Fighting broke out between the two and there were attacks by both Jewish and Arab terrorists on British troops and officials.

74

Towards Indian independence

The most serious signs of a popular movement for independence however, appeared in India. Soon after the First World War in which so many Indian soldiers had fought and died, the Indian National Congress, the main Hindu political organization, and the Moslem League decided to co-operate. Both wanted the self-government, which some English Liberals had been foreseeing since the 1850s, and independence if they could get it. The Government of India Act, 1919, aimed at establishing a parliamentary system with elected assemblies both in the provinces and at the Centre. The progress of the new Constitution was held up by violence and strikes. One tragic incident was at Amritsar when troops were ordered to fire upon an excited crowd, thought to be endangering European lives, and killed nearly 400 people. This caused passionate anti-British feelings. At intervals constitutional commissions investigated and reported, and eventually a Round Table Conference was called in London in 1930 to which leaders of all Indian parties were invited. The result of this was the Indian Act of 1935, according to which India was to be an independent Dominion within the Commonwealth as a federation of self-governing provinces. But, before the scheme could come into effect, a majority of the Rulers of Indian States would have to agree to it. Then came the Second World War.

Throughout this period the motive power for independence was Mahatma Gandhi (Mahatma means Holy One). As a young lawyer he had worked in South Africa on behalf of the Indian population. He returned to India after the First World War and proceeded to organize passive resistance to British rule in order to secure complete independence. He gave up wearing Western clothes, dressed in a loin-cloth and, himself working at a spinning wheel, he encouraged as many people as possible to return to the native crafts of their country. Unfortunately his boycotts and ignoring of laws, though starting with non-violence, ended in violence, so that Gandhi often found himself in prison. By 1939, however, it was clear that his ideal of complete national freedom would become sooner or later irresistible. Among those attracted by his teaching was a high-caste Brahmin from Kashmir, Pandit Nehru, who became his principal lieutenant.

Summary

After the First World War there was a great revival of pride in the British Empire, the 'Land of Hope and Glory'. The Empire contained all those countries described in Chapter 2, plus many territories taken from the defeated Germans and Turks.

These were administered as 'Mandates' under the League of Nations. They included Mesopotamia (Iraq), Jordan and Palestine in the Middle East; Tanganyika (German East Africa) and other African territories; South West Africa, administered by the South African Union as a part of the Empire; and islands in the Pacific.

There were two signs of change: 1 The Mandates were not permanent but were to be given up when the peoples of these countries were ready to govern themselves; the 'Dominions' – Canada, Australia, New Zealand and South Africa, as well as the Government of India – were recognized as separate, independent members of the League of Nations. Thus the seeds of independence for colonial peoples were sown.

The Statute of Westminster, 1931, described the British Commonwealth as an association of self-governing communities independent of one another, except for loyalty to the Crown. In this period Southern Ireland, ruled for centuries by England, became independent within the Commonwealth.

The Mandate for Iraq was given up. This started a general agitation for the independence of Egypt and other Arab countries. It also caused a violent Arab opposition to the Jews settling in Palestine.

The movement for Indian independence made great progress under the leadership of Mahatma Gandhi. It was agreed, before the Second World War broke out, that it should become a self-governing Dominion in the Commonwealth.

Chapter 12 *The challenge to democracy*

I THE ECLIPSE OF PARLIAMENTS

We are accustomed to look upon a parliament freely elected by all grown-up citizens as the right way of making and changing laws and controlling the government. So it is in countries where this system has its roots deep in history, and where loyalty to the nation is stronger than loyalty to party. England is nearly the oldest parliamentary country in the world (Iceland is the oldest). But in states in which the system of parliamentary government has not proved strong enough to overcome violent political, racial or tribal divisions or has failed for one reason or another to supply their basic needs (namely law and order, social justice, food, employment), the people have often turned against it. Parliament always means parties, seeking support for different policies and led by ambitious men. This is all very well when there are only two or three parties working within a single, established constitution. It does not work where there are lots of parties fighting for the profits of government jobs, or when a revolutionary minority will not accept the votes of the majority in parliament.

In these circumstances the strong man who comes forward as the national leader and promises to govern in the interests of all, has very often won great popular support. So it is not surprising today that nearly all newly independent African states, having started with parliamentary constitutions on the English or French model, have soon become single-party states under one political chief, or a military leader.

In Europe – apart from Soviet Russia where Stalin became an absolute dictator – this kind of 'authoritarian' rule appeared in the twenty years between the wars in every country except the constitutional monarchies of Britain, Scandinavia, Holland, Belgium and Luxembourg, and three Republics, France, Switzerland and Czechoslovakia. The real, or supposed, threat of Communism was usually one reason for this. In most cases parliamentary democracy was suspended or overthrown for particular national reasons without endangering other countries. But in Italy and Germany dictators arose who had aggressive ambitions with world-wide consequences. So did a group of militarists in Japan.

Some examples in Europe

Most of the European countries in which there were dictatorships or 'authoritarian' rulers before the Second World War are now controlled by Communist Parties, no less arbitrarily. In the western world there are three countries, Turkey, Portugal and Spain, in which the parliamentary system was discarded between the wars. In Turkey it has been restored, but with a good deal of violence between two contending parties. After the First World War a young General, Mustapha Kemal, refused to accept the humiliating Treaty of Sèvres. He raised an army, drove the Greeks, who had invaded Asia Minor, into the sea, deposed the Sultan and proclaimed a Republic in 1923. Though its constitution provided for representative government, only his own Republican People's Party was allowed. He was all powerful as President till he died in 1938. His aim was to transform the old Moslem Turkey into a modern secular state.

In Portugal the national revolution brought about by the Army in 1926 established a form of government without political parties which has not changed for forty-two years. The parliamentary system had in fact become ridiculous, with forty governments succeeding one another since the monarchy was abolished in 1910. Portugal was bankrupt: and it was primarily to put the national finances in order, that General Carmona, the leader of the National Revolution, persuaded Dr Salazar, a Professor of Economics, to become Prime Minister in 1932.[1] He succeeded. His government has been thrifty and authoritarian ever since; and Portugal has lived within its means without borrowing from other countries. Politics take second place to economics. A series of Development Plans are gradually industrializing the country. In the inter-war years there was hardly any of the present hostile foreign opinion about Portugal. This began with the outbreak of the anti-colonial campaign in 1960.

---

[1] He was replaced, after suffering a stroke, in 1968.

The Spanish Civil War

In Spain, unlike any other European country except Russia, the overthrow of the parliamentary system was the result of a terrible civil war.

Ever since the French Revolutionary Wars, Spain had been a sadly divided country. Lenin prophesied that Spain would be the next scene of a successful revolution after Russia.

The civil war of 1936 - 1939 was the last phase of a long fever. Social disorders increased after the First World War. There were violent strikes in 1921 as well as a financial crisis. Then the army stepped in. General Primo de Rivera denounced the bankruptcy of parliament and set up a Directory, mostly of Generals, which King Alphonso recognized as the government. Parliament was suspended, strikes prohibited and for a time there was a feeling of relief. But Primo was unable to invent any lasting system of government by the time he retired from the scene in 1930. Next year, with the usual revolutionary violence, a group of the Left Parties came to power and proclaimed a Republic. The King left the country but did not abdicate.

The Liberals in the new government announced various reforms but encountered relentless opposition from monarchists and conservatives. Thenceforward rival militant groups were organized, on the Right, the *Falange*, on the Left the revolutionary trade unions and workers' militia. The 1934 election was won by the conservatives, whereupon the Left started risings in Catalonia and the Asturias. In 1936 the various factions and syndicates of the Left grouped themselves in a 'Popular Front' and won the election. But the Government which they formed was unable to keep order amid a succession of strikes, church burnings, peasant revolts and assassinations of both Right and Left-wing leaders.

In July, 1936, General Franco crossed from Spanish Morocco, where the troops supported him, determined to overthrow the Popular Front and restore order. A number of garrisons in Spain – the majority of the regular army – rallied to his side; so did the Church, conservatives generally and the shock troops of the *Falange*.

But the supporters of the Government, especially the workers' militia, and a good part of the navy put up a most vigorous resistance, though quarrels between Communists and Anarchists weakened them. It took two years before the Nationalists, as General Franco's side was called, controlled all the south, west and north of the country, and Madrid did not fall to them till March 1939.

What aroused passionate feelings in many countries was the fact that Nazi Germany and Fascist Italy gave vigorous support with aircraft and troops to the Nationalists, while Soviet Russia helped the Republican Government. Most opinion in Britain, America and France was strongly against General Franco, and many volunteers joined the International Brigades organized by the Communists to fight him.

Nearly a million people were killed in this dreadful conflict between people of the same nation, and no Spaniard wants it to happen again. Many of the losing side fled into exile: others were imprisoned or executed. General Franco became the *Caudillo*, dictator of the country and head of state. The *Falange* was the only party or movement allowed. A Corporative system was announced but, before the long work of national reconstruction could make headway, the Second World War, in which Spain remained neutral, had broken out.

II THE AGGRESSIVE DICTATORS

Fascist Italy

Fasci means the bunch of rods tied round an axe, which was carried as an emblem of power by the *lictors*, officers attending the consuls of ancient Rome. It was used towards the end of the nineteenth century as the title of some revolutionary workers' organizations in Southern Italy.

Benito Mussolini started life as a school teacher and a revolutionary socialist, but quarrelled with the Socialist Party in 1914 because he was in favour of Italy coming into the war. He fought in it and was wounded. He revived *Fasci* as the name of a militant group, about 20,000 strong, which he founded in Milan in 1919. This was a mixture of unemployed ex-soldiers, anarchists, extreme nationalists and other misfits, united only by anger because Italy, they believed, had been cheated of the rewards of victory in the war, and by discontent at the chronic disorder of the country. Mussolini as their *Duce* (leader) played on these themes, the incompetence of the Liberals and Socialists in parliament and the danger of Bolshevism. His object was to capture power and make Italy great.

He organized his Fascists in military formations which would force their way to power by violence and terrorism. By 1921 the Fascists were over 300,000 strong. Mussolini was elected (on a joint list of government supporters and Fascists) as a member of parliament for Milan. Next year he was strong enough to thwart a general strike planned by the Communists, and led a 'march on Rome' at the head of his private army. In October 1922 King Victor Emmanuel, hoping to avoid violence, asked him to form a government.

From then on it was a quick progress to absolute power and the ruthless crushing of the opposition parties. Parliament became powerless; the Fascist Grand Council became, under the Duce, the one, all-powerful organ of the state, rather like the *Politburo* of the Communist Party in Russia. Bit by bit all the youth of the nation was mobilized, beginning with six-year old 'Children of the Wolf'. Next came the 'Balillas' (eight to fourteen), then the 'Avangardisti' (fourteen to eighteen), then the 'Young Fighting Fascists'. The motto was 'All for the State, nothing outside the State, nothing against the State'.

Until the early 1930s this intense nationalism seemed to carry no threat to other countries, and many foreigners were favourably impressed with the positive results of Fascism, in spite of the brutal way its opponents were treated. After all, the trains in Italy ran on time, and one was no longer fleeced by hotels, for prices were strictly fixed. There were no strikes. New roads, railways and hydroelectric schemes were built. Marshes were drained and farming developed.

Further, a running sore in Italian life was ended when peace was made between Pope Pius XI and the Italian Kingdom by the Lateran Treaty of 1929. The Papacy and the Kingdom had not been reconciled

How the world changed

since the seizure of Rome, the Papal capital, in 1870. Italy recognized the independent sovereignty of the Pope over a small symbolic state, the City of the Vatican, and a Concordat was signed by which the Catholic Church was recognized as the established church of Italy. This put an end to a conflict of loyalties in the hearts of most Italians. The Pope was much criticized for his reconciliation with the Fascist state and was soon in conflict with it about its domination of schools and youth organizations. But the benefits of the settlement were to be seen in the following years, first in the diplomatic independence of Pope Pius XII during the Second World War, then in the powerful encouragement which he gave the Catholic citizens to use their democratic rights when it ended.

It was the great World Depression (1929 - 1934), as we shall see, that really turned Fascist Italy into a menace to peace.

Nazi Germany

The German National Socialist Workers' Party (NAZI for short) was what Adolf Hitler called the small group which he formed to counteract Bolshevism among demobilized soldiers after the First World War. It had a similar origin and history to that of Mussolini's *Fascismo*. But it took longer to get off the ground and was from the first a danger to other countries. Hitler, who had been a corporal, wounded in the war, was a self-taught Austrian who, after a poor youth in Vienna, had volunteered in the Bavarian Army.

Like Mussolini, Hitler was a fanatical nationalist, and the aims of his new party were to provide work for all, to destroy the *Diktat* (Dictated Peace) of Versailles which had humiliated Germany, to 'free the country from the clutches of Jews, Marxists and foreigners' and make it all-powerful. Unemployment and the bitterness of defeat were the ground on which he built; but it was his insane belief in the Germans as the Master Race which gave his appeal its driving force. A para-military organization of riot squads called *Sturmabteilungen* (SA), or Storm troopers, was formed to support Hitler's little party and break up the meetings of his rivals. That was the beginning of the enormous armed gangs with which the party captured power. The

S A was displaced in importance by the S S, or Protection squads, in 1934. But in 1921 the Nazis only numbered 3,000 members.

The French occupation of the Ruhr in 1923 and the ruin caused that year by the crash of the German mark were seized upon by Hitler as the opportunity to start a 'National Revolution' in Munich. But his *Putsch* collapsed and he was sentenced to five years imprisonment. He was let out in six months, having used the time to write his book *Mein Kampf* (*'My Struggle'*). While street fighting between Nazis and Communists developed they both continued to seek election in parliament. In 1924 the Nazis still only won 2.8 per cent of the votes. It was the mass unemployment caused by the Great Depression that made them so powerful a party.

By playing on the danger of Communism and winning the support of monarchists and rich capitalists, Hitler became Chancellor (Prime Minister) in January 1933. In an election a few weeks later the Nazis won 44 per cent of the votes by terrorising their opponents, burning the *Reichstag* (Parliament) building and then accusing the Communists of doing it. In this way they prevented the Communists from taking their seats. In March Hitler was given Full Powers by the *Reichstag*, and next year, on the death of the old President, Field Marshal Hindenburg, he himself became President as well as Chancellor with the title *Reichsfuhrer* – Leader of the Empire. He was an absolute dictator.

THE CHALLENGE TO
THE PEACEFUL DEMOCRACIES

Three aggressive, dissatisfied governments, German, Japanese and Italian, were before long to challenge the satisfied and peaceful democratic countries to war. It is by seeing how each of them in turn successfully defied the League of Nations that we can best understand how the flash point was reached.

Manchuria

It began with Manchuria. By 1929 a militarist party was firmly in control in Japan. The fact that Japanese ambitions had been thwarted since the war, particularly by the United States, which now stopped all Japanese immigration, was one cause of this; another was the determination of the army leaders to crush all social discontent which the great Depression was making worse. Suddenly in 1931 the Japanese Army seized Manchuria from China. This coup succeeded so well and so quickly that it was followed by the conquest of more and more Chinese provinces. This was the first great defiance of the League, whose members ought, according to its Covenant, to have combined to defend China against this aggression. But the French and British Governments, and consequently the others, wriggled out of doing anything effective and the United States would do nothing to help.

Ethiopia

This gave Mussolini the green light. Hitherto he had been mainly concerned, as we have seen, with reorganizing Italy on Fascist lines. But the great Depression hit Italy badly. It stopped Italian emigration to the United States and so increased unemployment. To make up for economic difficulties at home, Mussolini needed some show of Italian grandeur abroad. So he proceeded to absorb the unemployed by building up a great army, revived the memories of Rome's imperial greatness, talked of the Mediterranean as *Mare Nostrum* (Our Sea) and looked for somewhere to conquer. He picked on Abyssinia, or Ethiopia as it is properly called, the mountainous Christian kingdom lying west of the two Italian colonies in East Africa – Eritrea and Somalia. The invasion of Ethiopia in the autumn of 1935 shocked the world; the more so as the Emperor of Ethiopia, Haile Selassie, had four times appealed to the League of Nations to prevent it. This was another flagrant breach of the Covenant. Under pressure, especially from opinion in Britain, the Council of the League condemned Italy as the aggressor and called for economic sanctions, that is the cutting off of trade with Italy. But the ban was only carried out in a half-hearted way by some, but not all, the members of the League. These sanctions being quite ineffective, members of the French and British governments realized that the resentment which they caused in Italy would only throw Mussolini – as it did next year – into the arms of Nazi Germany. A compromise was therefore secretly devised by M. Laval, the French Minister, and Sir Samuel Hoare, the British Foreign Secretary. When news of this leaked out, Sir Samuel Hoare was forced to resign by an immediate outcry in England. This did not prevent the accomplished fact. The Italian conquest was completed in May 1936 and before long recognized by the Powers.

Hitler's Gamble

This exhibition of weakness in turn gave the green light to Hitler, who had hitherto been cautious, knowing that British and French forces still greatly outnumbered the German. Having already started to rearm in defiance of the Versailles Treaty, he ordered the German Army to occupy the demilitarized Rhineland. This was in March 1936 while the Western countries were worried by the Ethiopian war. It was a violation both of the Versailles and Locarno Treaties. The German commanders had orders to withdraw if they met with any resistance. But there was none. The French and British peoples had no mind for war; the Belgians had already chosen neutrality. So Hitler met with nothing but feeble protests.

This was enough to convince him that, if he advanced step by step, he could get away with murder. His next stroke was to seize Austria in March 1938, after a long preparation of bullying and propaganda. Again there was no worthwhile opposition.

The Germans now nearly surrounded the Western and most populous part of Czechoslovakia, with its valuable armament works and other heavy industries. Hitler worked up a violent campaign of propaganda about the alleged ill-treatment of the Sudeten German minority by the Czechs (see Chapter 8) in the summer of 1938.

Appeasement

This really worried the governments in London and Paris, since Czechoslovakia had an alliance with France and appealed for help. Both governments, however, decided to buy peace, if they could, by attempting a compromise with Hitler. Mr Neville Chamberlain, the

How the world changed

British Prime Minister, took the initiative. He made three flights to see Hitler in Germany – at Godesberg, Berchtesgaden and Munich. On September 29th he was joined at Munich at his request by M. Daladier, the French Prime Minister, and Mussolini. They then agreed to advise the Czechs to hand over the Sudetenland to Germany, which, feeling utterly betrayed, the Czechs were obliged to do. The Germans occupied the Sudetenland, which included Czechoslovakia's main defences, on October 1st.

This act of 'appeasement' was very popular both in England and France. It seemed incredible to most people, especially those old enough to remember the First World War, that Germany would be so crazy as to plunge the world into war again. Not many people wanted to face the truth. Mr Winston Churchill, Mr Duff Cooper who resigned from the government, and most of the Labour Opposition in Parliament, demanded a policy of resistance to Hitler.

But it was now too late to stop him short of war. At best a breathing space had been gained in which to rearm. In March 1939 the Germans overran the whole of Czechoslovakia and seized Memel in Lithuania. Italy invaded and occupied Albania a few days later. Next, Hitler demanded Danzig and the Polish Corridor to the sea. He was evidently resolved on swallowing Poland; so at the eleventh hour Britain and France declared that if Poland were invaded, they would give it all the support in their power, which meant war. Hitler did not believe it.

The Nazi-Soviet Part

Thereupon the two great totalitarian powers, Germany and Soviet Russia, though deeply opposed to one another both nationally and in their political systems, decided, each for its own temporary reason, to do a deal and to divide Poland, Northern and Eastern Europe, between them. This pact, signed by the Russian and German Foreign Ministers, Molotov and Ribbentrop, in August 1939 triggered off the fatal war. On September 1st the German tanks poured into Poland. On September 3rd Britain and France (though in fact they gave no help to Poland) declared war on Nazi Germany.

Summary

In many European countries, people lost confidence in parliamentary democracy. This was generally when the government failed to 'deliver the goods' which the citizen needs (law and order, social justice, food, employment). This was the opportunity for the strong man to put himself forward as the national saviour.

Between 1929 and 1939 this happened in every European country, except the constitutional monarchies of Britain, Scandinavia and the Low Countries, and three republics, France, Switzerland and Czechoslovakia. In some countries, such as Turkey and Portugal, parliamentary democracy was suspended or overthrown for internal national reasons, without threatening other countries' independence.

In Spain there was a savage civil war from 1936 to 1939 as a result of which General Franco established a dictatorship. This caused passionate feelings in many countries, because Nazi Germany and Fascist Italy sent troops and aircraft to help him and the Nationalists, while Soviet Russia helped the defeated Republican Government.

Spain stayed neutral in the Second World War. But in three countries, where parliamentary democracy was suppressed, there arose dictators determined to conquer others. They were Germany, Italy and Japan.

Benito Mussolini in Italy and Adolf Hitler in Germany began soon after the First World War to organize parties of discontented young men in order to seize power. They were called *Fascists* in Italy, *National Socialists* in Germany. Both used parliamentary elections to obtain support but they won control by organized violence. Mussolini became head of the government in 1922. In spite of his extreme nationalism he did not seem to be a danger to other countries.

Hitler was more dangerous, because from the first he set out to undo the dictated Versailles Treaty and expand Germany's territory. Germans, he believed, were the 'Master Race'.

The World Economic Depression (1929 onwards) hit Germany and Italy, and also Japan. This helped Hitler and the Japanese militarists to increase their power. It made Mussolini look for grandeur outside Italy.

So began their challenge of the League of Nations. First in 1931 the Japanese seized Manchuria from China. This was a breach of the Covenant, but the British, French and other governments in the League failed to

How the world changed

stop them. This encouraged Mussolini in 1935 to conquer Ethiopia. The League made a half-hearted attempt to help Ethopia by stopping trade with Italy ('sanctions'), but it came to nothing.

This encouraged Hitler to move. In 1936 his troops occupied the Rhineland, breaking the Versailles Treaty; but France and Britain did nothing. So he continued bit by bit with his aggressive plan, seized Austria in 1938 and demanded the German-speaking part of Czechoslovakia.

The French and British Governments, anxious to prevent war, weakly agreed, though the French had a defensive alliance with the Czechs. Thereupon Hitler took the whole of Czechoslovakia.

Next he demanded the Polish Corridor to the sea, and Danzig. At last Britain and France realized that they must stand up to Nazi aggression, and so they promised Poland support. Stalin then decided to make his own terms with Hitler. Germany invaded Poland on September 1st, 1939; Britain and France declared war on Germany on September 3rd.

Suggested reading list for teachers

Note: some of the books published in the earlier years of the century are out of print but should be available in public libraries (F — *Fiction*)

General	*Our Times 1900 - 1960* Stephen King Hall. Faber and Faber
	The Last Hundred Years C. H. C. Blount. OUP
	Europe in the 19th and 20th Centuries A. J. Grant and H. Temperley. Longmans
	Recent History Atlas 1870 to the Present Day Gilbert Martin. Weidenfeld and Nicolson
	Living and Working: a Social and Economic History of England 1760 - 1960 L. F. Hobley. OUP

Part 1 1900 - 1914

Chapter 1	*Victoria RI* Elisabeth Longford. Weidenfeld and Nicolson
	Pax Britannica: the Climax of Empire James Morris. Faber and Faber
	A History of Everyday Things in England, Vol. 14, 1851 - 1914 Marjorie and C. H. B. Quennell. Batsford
	Bound volumes of *The Strand Magazine* and *Illustrated London News* in lending libraries
Chapter 2	*European Rule in Africa* A. J. Hanna. Historical Association
	The British Achievement in India H. G. Rawlinson. Pamphlet No. 46. Historical Association
	Four Guineas Elspeth Huxley. Chatto and Windus
	Russian Far Eastern Policy A. Malozennoff. University of California Press
	Russia John Lawrence. Methuen (historical survey)
	The American Story Ed. Earl Schenck Miers. Allen and Unwin

Chapter 3   *Rise of Modern China* Victor Purcell. Historical Association
Japan's Century R. F. Wall. Historical Association

Chapter 4   *The Struggle for Mastery in Europe 1848 - 1918* A. J. P.
Taylor. OUP
The Great Illusion Norman Angell
The European Anarchy G. Lowes Dickinson. Allen and
Unwin
(F) *The Riddle of the Sands* E. Childers. Pan
Twenty Years of Balkan Tangle Elizabeth Durham. Allen
and Unwin

Part 2 1914 - 1919

Chapter 5   *The Lamps Go Out: 1914 and Outbreak of War* A. F.
and 6   Alington. Faber and Faber
The First World War Cyril Falls. Longmans
Lloyd George C. L. Mowat and M. R. Price. OUP
World War I: an Illustrated History Ernest Benn
For Peace Settlement see *Europe in the 19th and 20th
Centuries*. Part V. A. J. Grant and H. Temperley. Long-
mans

Chapter 7   *A History of War and Peace* Wilfred Knapp
Ten Years' Life of the League of Nations (1919 - 1929) John
Eppstein. May Fair Press
(F) *Journey's End* (play) R. C. Sherriff. Heinemann Educa-
tional
(F) *All Quiet on the Western Front* E. M. Remarque. Mayflower
Books
(Forthcoming: 1968, Faber and Faber. World Outlook
1900 - 1965: a Study Series. *Struggle in the Deserts*
(Middle East from Lawrence to Nasser)

Part3 1919 - 1939

General   *Decade 1931 - 1941. A Commemorative Anthology* Hamish
Hamilton

Chapter 8 *From Peace to War: Europe 1918 - 39* M. G. Bruce. Thames and Hudson

The Lost Peace Harold Butler. Faber and Faber. (General Studies Library)

The Twenty Years Crisis 1919 - 39 E. H. Carr. Macmillan

Background to Eastern Europe F. B. Singleton. Pergamon Press

Chapter 9, *The Two Revolutions: an Eye-Witness Study of Russia, 1917* Bruce Lockhart. Bodley Head

The Bolshevik Revolution Alan Moorhead

Stalin Isaac Deutscher. OUP

(F) *And Quiet Flows the Don* M. Sholokhov. Putnam

Chapter 10 *Albert Einstein* Arthur Beckhard. A. & C. Black

The Man who discovered Penicillin (Sir Alexander Fleming) W. A. C. Bullock. Faber and Faber

The United States since the First World War C. P. Hill. Allen and Unwin

Britain's Locust Years 1918 - 1940 W. McElwee. Faber and Faber

Age of the Great Depression D. Wecter. Collier-Macmillan

History of the New Deal B. Rauch. Peter Smith

(F) *Love on the Dole* W. Greenwood. Cape

Chapter 11 *Commonwealth History* P. M. G. Bulmer. Blandford Press

Story of Gandhi Taya Zinkin. Methuen

Chapter 12 *Europe of the Dictators 1919 - 1945* Elisabeth Wiskemann. Collins

Rise and Fall of the Third Reich W. L. Shirer. Secker and Warburg

Mussolini and Italy C. C. Bayne-Jardine. Longmans

Portraits of Power S. E. Ayling. (17 leading personalities of the period.) Harraps

The Spanish Civil War Hugh Thomas. Eyre and Spottiswoode

The Grand Camouflage B. Bolloten. Introduction by H. R. Trevor Roper. Pall Mall Press

Failure of a Mission Sir Neville Henderson. Hodder and Stoughton

Is Innocence Enough? D. W. Brogan. Hamish Hamilton

Index

Abdullah, King   74
Afghanistan   13
Agadir   26
Alaska   11
Algeria   16
Allenby, General   36
Alliances, European   23–8
Alsace-Lorraine   41
Anarchists   6, 80
Anglo-Irish Treaty (1921)   73
Anglo-Japanese Alliance   12, 21
Anglo-Russian Convention   26
Angola   15
Arabs   38, 74
Armaments, race in   25
Armistice (Nov. 1918)   40
Australia   13, 72
Austria   24, 27, 33, 41

Balfour Declaration   37
Balkan Wars   23, 27
Bankruptcies of German banks   67–8
BBC   63
Bechuanaland   14
Bela Kun   49
Belgium, invasion of   28, 33
Benguela Railway   15
Benedict XV, Pope   39
Berlin Conference (1885)   9
Bismarck   3, 24, 47
Blockade, British   35
Boer War   1, 13
Bolsheviks   37, 53, 81, 82
Brest Litovsk, Treaty of   37
Briand, Monsieur   45
Britain   6, 7, 9, 33, 42, 64–5, 86
British Empire   33; and Commonwealth   69–76
Bulgaria   23, 33, 40

Canada   11, 13, 72
Carmona, General   78
Cecil, Lord Robert   44
Central Powers (First World War)   33
Chamberlain, Sir Austen   45
Chamberlain, Neville   85
Chaplin, Charlie   63
China   19–21, 84
Chinese Empire   9; Boxer Rising   12
Chinese Revolution   19
Churchill, Winston   74, 86
Cinema industry, American   62
Clémençeau   39, 42
Collins, Michael   74
Commonwealth PM Conferences   75
Communist International   59
Communist Parties   57–9, 78, 80, 81, 83
'Concert of Europe'   17, 23
Congo   11
Conservative Party, British   6
Counter-revolutionaries, Russian   56
Court of International Justice   45
Cuba   12
Czar, Nicholas II   22, 53
Czechoslovakia   41, 44, 49, 71, 85

Daladier   86
Danzig   86
Dardenelles   35
Dead, in First World War   40
Democracy   31
Democratic Party (USA)   43
Devaluation of currencies (1931)   67
Disney, Walt   63
Dreadnoughts   26

Dreyfus, Captain 3
Dutch Empire 16

East African Campaign (1914–18) 33
Economics (between World Wars) 64–8
Economics of the Commonwealth 72–3
Edward VII, King 2, 25
Entente (First World War) 33
Entente Cordiale 15, 25
Esthonia 49
Ethiopia, invasion of (1935) 84–5
Europe, new map of 47–8

Falange 79, 80
Fascist Italy 80–5
Finland 49
Five-year Plans (USSR) 58
Fleming, Sir Alexander 62
Foch, Marshal 34, 39
France 2, 24, 33, 77
Franco, General 79, 80
Franco-British Naval Convention 26
Franz Ferdinand, Crown Prince 27
French Empire 16

Gandhi, Mahatma 75
'Gay 'twenties' 61
George V, King 22, 28
German colonies 17
Germany 3, 9, 24–8, 41
Goa 15
Gold standard 65
Greece 23, 39
'Green Europe' 4
Grey, Sir Edward 23, 27–8

Hague Conferences 22
Haig, General 39
Haile Selassie, Emperor 84

Hapsburg Monarchy, dismembered 47
Hawaii 12
Hindenburg, Field Marshal 83
Hitler, Adolf 45, 60, 68, 82–3
Hoare, Sir Samuel 85
Holland 9
Horthy, Admiral 49
Hungary 27, 41

Iceland 77
Imperialism 1; American 11; Russian 12; British 13
Imperial Preferences 65, 73
India 11, 13, 75
Indian National Congress 75
Indochina 16
International Labour Organization 45
Iraq, independence of 74
Ireland, Easter Rising (1916) 35
Irish Free State 72
Irish Republic 74
Italy 6, 24, 17, 33

Japan 9, 20, 21, 33, 82
Jewish National Home 37, 38, 74
Jews 82
Joffre, General 34
Johnson, Amy 62
Jutland, Battle of 35

Kemal Ataturk 41, 78
Kerensky 53
Kolkoz 58
Kuomintang 20

Labour Party, British 6, 65, 86
Lateran Treaty 81
Latvia 49
Laval 85
League of Nations 44, 45, 51, 59, 72, 84

Lebanon 16
Lenin 53–7, 79
Leo XIII, Pope 23
Leopold II, King 9, 11
Lindbergh, Colonel 62
Litvinoff 59
Lloyd George 27, 39, 42, 74
Locarno, Treaty of 45
Lourenço Marques 15
Ludendorff, General 39

Malay States 73
Manchu dynasty 19
Manchuria 12, 21, 83
Mandates 45, 70, 71
Marne, Battle of the 34
Marx Karl 6
Marxism-Leninism 57
Mein Kampf 83
Mesopotamia 13
Mexico 11
Minorities 50; Treaties 51
Moltke, General 27
'Monroe Doctrine' 11
Montenegro 50
Morocco 16, 25, 26
Moslem League 75
Mozambique 15
Munich Conference 86
Mussolini, Benito 80, 81, 82, 86

Nationalism 31, 81
National self-determination 50
National Socialists (Nazis) 66, 68, 82–3
Nazi Germany 80, 82–3
Nazi-Soviet Pact 86
Nehru, Pandit 76
NEP 57–8
'New Deal', Roosevelt's 67–8
Newfoundland 72
New Zealand 13, 72

Nigeria 11
Nyasaland (Malawi) 14

Olympic Games 63
Orthodox Church 58
Ottoman Empire 16, 23

Panama Canal 12
Paris 34; Peace Conference 41
Peace Movement, weakness of 22
Peace Treaties, Versailles: St Germain; Neuilly; Trianon; Sèvres; Lausanne 41
Penicillin 62
Persian Gulf 6
Philippines 12
Pius XI, Pope 81
Poland 41, 44, 49, 86
'Popular Front' 79
Portugal 6, 9, 33, 78
Portuguese Empire 14, 15
Primo de Rivera, General 79
Puerto Rico 12

Quebec 13

Rapallo, Treaty of 59
Reichstag 38, 83
Reparations 42, 43, 66
Rhineland 43, 46, 85
Rhodes, Cecil 14
Rhodesia 14, 16
Roman Catholic Church 37, 82
Roosevelt, President Franklin 67
Roosevelt, President Theodore 12
Ruanda-Urundi 17
Ruhr, occupation of 44, 83
Rumania 23, 33, 40, 41, 44, 49
Russia 24, 27, 33, 34, 49
Russian Revolution 37, 43, 52–7
Russo-Japanese War 21

Saar plebiscite 51
Sanctions, economic 84
Sarajevo 27
Serbia 23, 27, 33
Smuts, General 44, 71
Social Democrats 23
Socialism 6
Somme, Battle of the 35
South Africa 13, 14, 72
South Slavs 27
Soviet Union 52–60
Spain 6, 9, 12, 78–9
Spanish Civil War 79–80
Stalin 56–8, 77
Stresemann, Herr 45
Sudan, Anglo-Egyptian 14
Sudeten Germans 85–6
Submarines, German 35, 37
Sun Yat-sen 19, 20
Switzerland 77
Syria 16

Tanganyika 15, 17
Tannenberg, Battle of 34
Tennessee Valley Authority 67
Total war 32
Trade Union Congress (British) 38
Trans-Siberian Railway 12
Transylvania 33, 40, 50
Trench warfare 34
'Trojan Horse' tactics 59

Trotsky 56
Tunisia 16
Turkey 17, 33, 78

Uganda 14
Ukraine 49
Unemployment in Britian 42, 64,
    65; USA 67; Germany 68, 83;
    Italy 84
United States 5, 37, 66–8

Vatican, City 81
Verdun 35
Victor Emmanuel, King 81
Victoria, Queen 1, 2, 25
Vladivostok 12

Wall Street Crash (1929) 66
Westminster, Statute of (1931) 72
William II, Kaiser 3, 46
Wilson, President 37, 39, 42–4
World War, First 22–7; 31–41

Yuan Shih-kai 20
Yugoslavia 41, 44, 50

Zanzibar 14
Zionists 35

CA AND ASIA IN 1968

Names underlined indicate government by Europeans.

Ingram Content Group UK Ltd.
Milton Keynes UK
UKHW051146030423
419467UK00021B/647